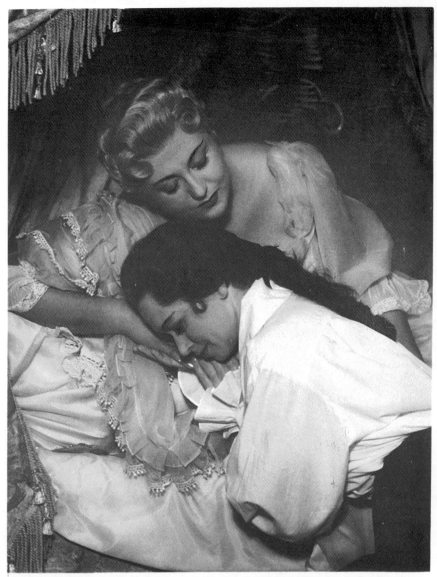

Régine Crespin as the Marschallin and Elisabeth Söderström as Octavian in Carl Ebert's production, designed by Oliver Messel, at Glyndebourne, 1959. (photo: Guy Gravett)

Der Rosenkavalier

Richard Strauss

Opera Guide Series Editor: Nicholas John

Calder Publications Limited
Riverrrun Press Inc.
Paris · London · New York

Published in association with English National Opera

COPYRIGHT DATA

First published in Great Britain, 1981,
by Calder Publications Limited
9-15 Neal Street, London WC2H 9TU

First published in the U.S.A., 1981, by
Riverrun Press Inc., 1170 Broadway,
New York, NY 10001

ISBN 0 7145 4268 7

BRITISH LIBRARY CATALOGUING IN PUBLICATION DATA
Der Rosenkavalier — (Opera guide; 8)
  1. Strauss, Richard. Rosenkavalier
  2. Operas — Librettos
  I. Strauss, Richard   II. Hofmannsthal, Hugo von
  III. John, Nicholas   IV. Series
  782.1'092'4   ML410.S93

English National Opera receives financial assistance from the Arts Council of
Great Britain.

Typeset in Plantin by Spooner Typesetting & Graphics, London NW5.
Printed and bound in Great Britain.

CONTENTS

LIST OF ILLUSTRATIONS

An Introduction to 'Der Rosenkavalier'

Derrick Puffett

In Iris Murdoch's novel *The Black Prince*, the narrator goes to a performance of *Der Rosenkavalier*. 'The curtain suddenly fled away to reveal an enormous double bed surrounded by a cavern of looped-up blood-red hangings ... two girls were lying in a close embrace. (At least I suppose one of them was enacting a young man.) Then they began to sing ... The two women were conversing in pure sound, their voices circling, replying, blending, creating a trembling silver cage of an almost obscene sweetness ... these were not words but the highest coinage of human speech melted down, become pure song, something vilely almost murderously gorgeous ... I was definitely going to be sick.'

Any newcomer to *Der Rosenkavalier* may experience some — one hopes, not all! — of these sensations. In the novel, it is true, they are not produced exclusively by the music; but Murdoch's language — 'an almost obscene sweetness ... vilely almost murderously gorgeous' — captures the work's immense physical power, its ability to attract and repel. What *is* it, this astonishing mixture of sentimentality and voluptuousness, of coarse good humour and tender naivety, of manners 'wholly Viennese' (Hofmannsthal) and emotions familiar to us all? After an orchestral prelude which is probably music's most graphic depiction of lovemaking — Strauss tried to surpass it in *Arabella*, but there the music is not so good — he gives us not only Octavian and the Marschallin but Ochs, Sophie, Faninal, an Italian intriguer and his

Anne Evans (the Marschallin) and Josephine Barstow (Octavian). (photo: John Garner)

7

accomplice (not to mention Ochs's lackeys, ancestors of Macheath's thugs in *The Threepenny Opera*, the Three Noble Orphans, waiters, musicians and pantomime trapdoors. All in music ranging from pastiche rococo (Ochs's first entry) to pastiche Expressionism (his humiliation) and taking in, between the two extremes, the various types of music associated with Octavian, Sophie and the Marschallin.

First some cold facts. Strauss met Hofmannsthal in 1900; but their collaboration did not begin until five years later, when the poet approached the composer with the idea of turning his play *Elektra* into an opera. As they worked together, Strauss's respect for Hofmannsthal grew: 'We were born for one another', he wrote. Even before the *Elektra* première, which took place on January 25, 1909, they were discussing future projects. At that time Hofmannsthal was preoccupied with French literature of the 17th and 18th centuries; also with the characters of Mozart's *Figaro*. Then on February 11 he sent Strauss the 'scenario for an opera, full of burlesque situations and characters, with lively action, pellucid almost like a pantomime . . . It contains two big parts, one for baritone and another for a graceful girl dressed up as a man, à la Farrar[1] or Mary Garden[2]. Period: the old Vienna under the Empress Maria Theresa.'

This was the nucleus of *Der Rosenkavalier* (or *Ochs von Lerchenau*, as they came to think of it: the title was changed only four months before the première). Work advanced rapidly, and soon Hofmannsthal suggested: 'Do try and think of an old-fashioned Viennese waltz, sweet and yet saucy, which must pervade the whole of the last act'. The last act, as we know, was the one that gave Strauss the most problems; for whereas he was able to compose the music for the first two almost concurrently with the writing of the text (with some reshaping in the case of the second, it is true), he received the words for Act Three over a much longer period and thus had a correspondingly less secure grasp of the total shape. One reason for the delay was that Hofmannsthal was worrying about the character of the Marschallin. As she increased in importance, the work lost some of its intended lightness, and so (to paraphrase Norman Del Mar, author of the standard English study of Strauss) the 'Pantomime with opportunities even for a short ballet' turned into a 'gay, cheerful, but profoundly psychological drama'. Once Strauss had the full text, however, composition proceeded swiftly. The première, a brilliant success, took place on January 26, 1911 at the Dresden Court Opera.

*

Four months later, on May 18, Mahler died (he had been brought back ill from New York without having heard the new opera). Strauss wrote to Hofmannsthal: 'Mahler's death has been a great shock to me'. At around the same time he wrote in his diary: 'I want to call my *Alpine Symphony* the "Antichrist", for it portrays moral purification through one's own strength, freedom through work, and worship of eternal, glorious nature!'

What do these remarks mean? That Strauss had been reading Nietzsche, to be sure, but what else? They sound unlike Strauss, somehow; more like

1. Geraldine Farrar (1882-1967), American soprano who made her début at the Berlin Court Opera in 1901.
2. Mary Garden (1874-1967), Scottish soprano who created the rôle of Mélisande in Debussy's *Pelléas et Mélisande* in Paris in 1902.

Mahler — the Mahler of the letters or the Third Symphony. And freedom from what? Strauss had met Mahler in 1887, when both were in their twenties. From then until Mahler left for America (1907) their work brought them into occasional contact with each other. According to Del Mar, Strauss's opinion of Mahler was typical of the time: 'That's really no composer at all. Just a very great conductor.' But his music suggests otherwise. In the early tone poems, notably *Don Quixote*, there are passages which may well have influenced Mahler, but after about 1900 the influence seems to be going the other way. Two Strauss works in particular, *Symphonia Domestica* and the *Alpine Symphony* (the latter not finished till 1915), suggest a musical obsession with Mahler; apart from the many cross-references, they were his last and longest tone poems and the only two to be called 'symphony'. Surely with two such near-contemporaries, both composer-conductors working in related fields of instrumental music, there must have been feelings of rivalry? Can one not detect in Strauss's diary entry, written in reaction to Mahler's death, even some spirit of relief?

Even during Mahler's lifetime, however, Strauss had, so it seems, tried to free himself from the other's influence, mainly by moving out of their common field: in opera Mahler could influence him only as a conductor. There is little Mahler in *Salome* or *Elektra*; on the contrary, Strauss's imagination seems to be burning more brightly than ever. But between *Elektra* and the *Alpine Symphony* comes *Rosenkavalier*. The opera is less obviously affected by Mahler than the symphonies, as we should expect. But there are two passages — and they are two of the most famous — which seem to me profoundly Mahlerian: the passage in which the Marschallin describes how she gets up at night and stops the clocks (harp harmonics, a favourite Mahlerian sonority), and the passage concerning her Uncle Greifenklau. It is interesting that both passages serve to suggest a dimension beyond the immediate dramatic context. The idea of 'time standing still' was to become a preoccupation, almost a cliché, with the composers of the next generation, composers such as Berg and Schreker; their works show they remembered this passage musically, too. And the whole point about Uncle Greifenklau, the sick old man whom the Marschallin visits, is that he never appears in person: he is used to evoke a whole world of social interaction, a world which by its very nature cannot be represented on stage. The string theme, half-lamenting, half-aspiring ('one eye wet, one dry!' as Strauss told a singer), which accompanies the Marschallin at this moment is intensely Mahlerian: one wonders whether Uncle Greifenklau was not also Director of the Vienna Court Opera.

Now why all this Mahlerising? Because I want to get closer to what *Rosenkavalier* is, and one way of doing this is by showing what it is not. For whatever else it is, it is not a 'staged tone poem' — a cliché often applied to *Salome* and *Elektra*. This cliché seems to go back to Ernest Newman, but survives in all sorts of places, even the *New Grove*, which goes so far as to call *Salome* 'a tone poem with vocal interludes'. It is misleading, on the one hand because it means ignoring the drama, on the other because it implies a false idea of what the tone poem had become. 'Symphonic writing', after Mahler, means a breakdown of the music into motifs, a constant variation of these motifs and an aural explanation of how these things are done, the last being provided through the orchestration — which thus becomes a more essential part of the composition than ever before. The orchestration in fact *is* the composition. Now as soon as we compare Mahler and Strauss in any detail we see that they are not really similar at all (and so not strictly comparable). It is

Risë Stevens as Octavian — a much admired interpretation for many years at the Metropolitan from 1938. (Covent Garden Archives)

largely a matter of texture. Whereas Strauss — for instance in the 'Uncle Greifenklau' section — tends to be homophonic (melody plus chordal accompaniment), in Mahler the texture is often so fragmented that it is hard to tell what 'melody' and 'accompaniment' mean. Their attitudes are symbolised in their respective treatments of the waltz: whereas Mahler builds it up, distorts it and makes it more complex, Strauss simplifies it, purifies it and indeed gives it back something of its pre-Mahlerian character. (This is perhaps too great a generalisation for *Rosenkavalier*, where one finds every possible kind of waltz, from the most sublimated — the Trio! — to the most vulgarised.)

So the work is not a tone poem. It is not, except for a few, rather untypical passages, music drama either — to the extent that 'music drama' is equated with late Wagner. True, it has leitmotifs, but they are nearly all melodic; there is none of the density, none of the rapid succession of textures and tone-colours, that we find in late Wagner, where 'motif' means harmony or timbre as often as it means melodic line. And the 'highlights' of the opera, its 'great moments' — the Marschallin's monologue, the Presentation of the Silver Rose, the Trio — are pure lyricism. Strauss loved the sound of the soprano voice, and here we hear it again and again — solo, à 2 and à 3. Hofmannsthal, who came out with all sorts of criticisms of the work after it was complete (he made the present point in 1928), thought that 'the life of the whole thing is centred on the orchestra'. But though the orchestra often has the tune, the tune is more lyrical than is customary in Wagner, and as likely as not it will already have been heard in a vocal part. Again it is a matter of texture. The texture of *Rosenkavalier* — of its 'highlights', anyway — is closer to Mozart, or Verdi, or Tchaikovsky, than it is to Wagner; and if one looks for a passage in which the orchestra is given its head — as in the *Feuersnot* love scene, or Elektra's last waltz, or Daphne's transformation — the closest one gets is the Trio, where the voices are used as extra stops on a vast organ, everything doubling everything else. In *Rosenkavalier*, ultimately, the voice dominates.

Is it number opera, then? No, because it is still continuous. Operetta? Hardly. What *Rosenkavalier* is, if it can be tied down so specifically, is a hybrid of all these things: number opera for the set pieces, music drama for the transitions, operetta for quite extended sections (notably the end of Act Two and the beginning of Act Three). At some points it even breaks down into accompanied speech. Texture, pace, tone are constantly changing — sometimes with a bump, as on the third-act entry of the Marschallin — but these very changes, which make the work so hard to define, are also part of its fascination.

*

Now we have a better idea of what it is, we can look at some of the critical orthodoxies surrounding it. The most uncritical of these critical views, indeed the most banal of all banalities about Strauss, is that it constitutes a 'retreat' from the discoveries of *Salome* and *Elektra*. This view must be seen in its historical context. It originated with Schoenberg and his followers, who regarded Strauss as having deserted the modernist cause at a crucial time. It would be a distortion of Schoenberg's views to say he thought there was only one way for music to go (i.e. his way); but that is the assumption underlying the hostility to *Rosenkavalier*. If we look at *Salome* and *Elektra* more carefully, we find that the 'modernism' is largely surface, the instant response to a poetic

11

idea. Wherever the texture is continuous — as in Salome's Dance, or the *Elektra* Recognition Scene, or the whole waltz-finale — it is as simple, and the harmony often as diatonic, as anything in *Rosenkavalier*. We think of *Salome* and *Elektra* as 'modern' works, with little islands of vocal beauty amid the chromatic turmoil. But we can also think of them (and it becomes easier to do so as the years go by) as giant puff pastries with occasional ventures into modernism. If we do, *Rosenkavalier* emerges as part of a continuous process, a process of purification which had begun long before the *Alpine Symphony*. 'Purification' here means self-discovery, deciding what one can do best, freeing oneself of unwanted influences. There is a letter from Strauss to Hofmannsthal (1916) in which he writes: 'I feel downright called upon to become the Offenbach of the 20th century . . . Sentimentality and parody are the sensations to which my talent responds most forcefully and productively'. If we think back to the tone poems we realise this was true all along: *Don Juan*, *Don Quixote* and *Till* are the most successful. In the operatic field, *Feuersnot* (but musically it is uneven), then nothing till *Rosenkavalier, Ariadne*, etc. From this point of view *Salome* and *Elektra* — and, looking ahead, even such a work as *Die Frau ohne Schatten* — appear as marvellous distractions, diversions from what Strauss was really best suited to do.

Rosenkavalier, where sentimentality and parody are of the essence, puts him back on course: for 'retreat' read 'advance'! After *Ariadne* there is the *Bourgeois gentilhomme* music, *Arabella, Capriccio* and the late instrumental works. Finally come the *Four Last Songs*, in which sentimentality is 'raised to the level of great art'. The question here is not whether sentimentality and parody are worthy concerns in themselves, merely whether they were right for Strauss. Surely the works prove they were. If we take the Schoenbergian line we end up saying that everything Strauss wrote after *Elektra* constitutes a 40-year decline, followed by the inexplicable miracle of the *Four Last Songs*. This is not very helpful. If on the other hand we view his work as a continuous process of purification, a discovering of opportunities to use those particular resources with which he was so well endowed (in this context we could almost call them 'gifts'), then there is no problem. The 'simplicities' of *Rosenkavalier* — the clear textures, the diatonic harmonies, the vocal domination, the sheer *enjoyability* of the thing — these are all part of a progress to the late songs.

Rosenkavalier has, nevertheless, been abused pretty consistently over the years, though not by the general public. 'All we find . . . is a worn-out, dissipated *demi-mondaine*, with powdered face, rouged lips, false hair, and a hideous smile. Strauss's music has lost her chastity' (Cecil Gray, writing in 1924). 'Strauss's most cynical, most rambling and most repetitive work in proportion to its length' (William Austin, 1966). Times have changed, but not the tone. Here it seems more profitable to see what the two authors of the work had to say about it after its success. Hofmannsthal was always making criticisms. In a single letter of 1916 he faults Strauss's treatment of a chorus in Act Two, his music for the servants at the end of Act One, and the Baron's final exit. Twelve years later he dismisses the whole libretto ('the one engaging character, the Marschallin, disappears for an act and a half and is only dragged in with difficulty at the end; the *buffo* a garrulous and repulsive fellow; the third act most superficially tacked on to the second', etc.); and three weeks before his death he refers to the 'weakish third act'. In more positive mood, however, he recognised its 'charm', that 'special *brio*' which results from 'the concentration of colourful contrasts and incidents in each separate act' — Act Two being cited as an example. Strauss of course loved the work; but he

Richard Mayr who created the role of Ochs in Vienna (but not in Dresden). Strauss once told him that he imagined him all the time in the role. Mayr asked whether that was really a compliment or an insult! Ernest Newman described his performance at Covent Garden in 1924, 'His smile and whistle during Annina's reading of the letter said more than a page of words could have done.'

recognised its longueurs, and made cuts when he performed it. He saw clearly that 'apart from the misunderstood waltz [it had been attacked as anachronistic], the success of *Rosenkavalier* was in the entry of the Rose Bearer, the end of Act One, and the Trio!' (letter to Hofmannsthal of 1928). Both seemed to regard the work as their most successful collaboration.

What is interesting here is that, while both men understood perfectly where the work succeeded, they were less clear about where it went wrong. Hofmannsthal's remarks still bear traces of those confusions which caused the problems in the first place. Audiences are not unduly bothered by the chorus in Act Two, and the servants in Act One are a positive delight. The Baron's exit is bad, but this is the fault of the libretto as much as the music. The third act is indeed weak (Hofmannsthal's changing conception of the Marschallin was a factor here), but is the second very much better? Hofmannsthal cites it for its 'concentration', but it can seem ramshackle. Putting all these points together one sees the emergence of a pattern: that of a strong first act (ending with a reflective monologue), a weaker second and a recovery in the third. This pattern reproduces itself in *Die Frau ohne Schatten, Arabella* and *Die Liebe der Danae*; and since the last is not to a Hofmannsthal text one must look for the explanation in Strauss. Perhaps it is simply that, being primarily a lyrical composer, he excels in music of exposition and reflection rather than in music of development and elaboration: had he written the *Ring, Das Rheingold* would have been musically superior to *Die Walküre*. He has a strong sense of climax,

13

Alfred Roller's designs were approved by Strauss and Hofmannsthal and opera houses were for years obliged to adopt the designs if they wanted to stage the opera. The sets were seen at Covent Garden in 1936 on the visit of the Dresden State Opera Company.

so his endings always work; but he is not so infallible in the preparation. The low-point usually comes about halfway through Act Three, when (perhaps in compensation) the music is at its busiest: Ochs's humiliation in *Rosenkavalier*, the comings and goings in *Die Frau*. Then comes the dénouement, things settle down, and Strauss is safe.

That there are 'problems' with *Rosenkavalier* not even its most ardent admirer would doubt. Perhaps — for these are not matters that can be tested — the plot is too thin for a work of such length. Perhaps the busyness of the action, the large number of characters, etc., are manifestations of this thinness (Hofmannsthal's equivalent of Strauss filling the texture with notes). Or perhaps the work simply falls between too many stools: the plot calls for the lightness of operetta; 'music drama' holds up the pace; but Strauss needs the continuity of music drama for the suavity and opulence of the set pieces — themselves a bow to number opera. Of course as soon as one says all this one realises that *Rosenkavalier* is what it is, that the stylistic joltings are part of its character, indeed essential to it; that the causes of its weakness are also the causes of its fascination. The positive side of the coin is this. If *Rosenkavalier* hardly works as a whole, it is full of moments which seem to appeal to the listener in a directly personal way. It teems with memorable lines and phrases (from this point of view it is the opera-goer's *Hamlet*); and everyone has his or her favourite passage. It is surely this personal element — the feeling that the listener is being wooed, or cajoled, as well as being taken by force (Iris Murdoch's character sensed only the latter) — that accounts for its lasting success.

Comedy for Music

Michael Kennedy

'This is no music for me', said Kaiser Wilhelm II as he left a performance of the new opera by his court conductor Richard Strauss in Berlin. He was in the minority then and has remained in it ever since, for *Der Rosenkavalier (The Knight of the Rose*, or, better, *The Rose-Bearer)* was an enormous and widely publicised success on its first performance at Dresden on January 26, 1911 and has since become an indispensable part of the repertoire of every opera company which aspires to international standards. True, Vienna at first ran to form and was not too sure about it, while the waltzes upset the first Milan audience, but London took it to its heart straightaway when Beecham conducted the first British performance at Covent Garden on January 29, 1913. The reasons for its success are not hard to define. It is a good story, of young love, of lustful love and of sacrificial love; it is melodious; it is spectacular; it combines Wagnerian richness with Mozartian elegance and a *Fledermaus*-Straussian waltzing gaiety; it is witty, touching, bawdy and broadly comic; its principal characters are so real that audiences feel they know them and identify with them as well as they know and identify with Shakespearean characters or those in *The Mastersingers of Nuremberg* and *The Marriage of Figaro*; it deals with high life and low life intermixed; and, by anachronistic musical means, it nostalgically captures an era, for although ostensibly about mid-eighteenth-century Vienna, it is also about the world of 1910, just before the First World War changed it forever. As the late Sir Neville Cardus wrote so tellingly, 'imagination can hear time running out like sand during the performance of *Der Rosenkavalier* in a great opera house at the height of a season.'

This last 'social' aspect of *Der Rosenkavalier* has an important *raison d'être*; it was the last convincing operatic comedy of manners which could ever be written, the last opera of dalliance and intrigue of an aristocratic provenance, because Strauss was the last musician of any importance who worked as a court *Kapellmeister* — at Meiningen, Munich, Weimar and Berlin — and who understood the structures and traditions of that vanishing world. (He composed three autobiographies of his *Kapellmeister* life, the orchestral tone-poem *Ein Heldenleben*, and the operas *Der Rosenkavalier* and *Ariadne auf Naxos*.) It is not surprising that Strauss should have seized upon Hofmannsthal's libretto with such enthusiasm. When Hofmannsthal first described the plot to him, Strauss exclaimed, 'We'll go ahead with this. You go straight home and send Act One as soon as you can.' At certain points, Strauss composed the music for certain dramatic situations *before* he received the libretto (he even composed a stage direction by mistake!)[1]. That tells us how vividly he saw the work in his mind. And, as will be seen, the opera's most theatrically effective *coups* were nearly all Strauss's ideas. Hofmannsthal acknowledged that the composer had taught him 'a fundamental lesson in writing dramatically for music which I shall not forget'.

Der Rosenkavalier, Strauss's Opus 59, is scored for a very large orchestra, thus: 3 flutes (3rd playing piccolo); 3 oboes (3rd playing cor anglais); 3 clarinets; bass clarinet (also basset-horn); 4 horns; 3 trumpets; 3 trombones;

---

1. 'with discreet secrecy'

15

bass tuba; timpani, bass drum, cymbals, triangle, tambourine, glockenspiel, tenor drum, side drum, bells, castanets, celesta; 2 harps; 16 first and 16 second violins, 12 violas, 10 cellos and 8 double basses. There is also an offstage orchestra in Act Three. Before the first performance in Dresden there were 22 orchestral rehearsals. Strauss directs the conductor to reduce the number of strings in passages 'where the audibility of the words requires it'. His whole operatic career was devoted to perfecting a technique whereby the words were audible to the listeners, whatever the size of the orchestra. He was, after all, working with librettists whose words were usually well worth hearing, particularly in the case of Hofmannsthal. The parallel with *The Marriage of Figaro* extends to the casting: three of the principal roles are sung by three sopranos, the role of Octavian being a *travesti* role in the Vienna tradition (comparable to the page Cherubino in Mozart). The principal male singers are baritones or basses, with the tenor reserved for a subsidiary *buffo* part. Hofmannsthal, like da Ponte, gives an extra twist to the sexual equivocation of the *travesti* part by making the character impersonate a woman: thus a woman dressed as a man has to dress as a woman. It is interesting to note that the *travesti* role in *Der Rosenkavalier* was Hofmannsthal's idea but when Strauss decided to repeat the formula in the Prologue to *Ariadne auf Naxos* and to give the role of the young Composer to a woman, Hofmannsthal was horrified. In their last collaboration, *Arabella*, the heroine's sister Zdenka passes most of the opera dressed as a boy, a deception insisted on by her impoverished parents because they cannot afford the expense of marrying off two daughters.

Act One

The opera begins with an orchestral Introduction which tells the audience unmistakably what is happening behind the not-yet-risen curtain — that a couple are making vigorous, passionate and mutually satisfying love[2]. The priapic import of the thrusting horns can scarcely be disguised. Nor has a more sensuous 'afterglow' ever been composed for strings. But haven't we heard something very like it before? Yes; Strauss's tone poem *Don Juan*. This Introduction opens with the leitmotif [1] which represents the Rosenkavalier himself, Count Octavian Rofrano, aged 17 years and two months at this point in the early years of the reign of Empress Maria Theresa of Austria. It is scored for four horns in E, with three bassoons and pizzicato cellos and basses. Understandably in the circumstances, it is marked *Con moto agitato*. This is immediately followed by [2] on strings, horns and woodwind, in the alien key of E flat major, almost immediately going into the tonic key of E major by means of Strauss's favourite device of a chromatic sideslip. The point of mentioning this technicality is that the listener will respond, perhaps without knowing the musical reason why, to the abrupt differentiation of character. [2] is the first of several themes to be associated with the Marschallin, or to give her her full title Die Feldmarschallin Fürstin Werdenberg (the wife of the Field Marshal Prince von Werdenberg). Now — and we are only in the fifth bar —comes another Octavian theme, [3], and, three bars later, yet another, [4], which is marked not only *agitato* but 'very extravagant in execution' (*sehr überschwenglich im Vortrag*). As the excitement grows, with trills for flutes, the

---

2. Illustrations on pp 37/8 show how differently from early productions this scene can now be staged.

D clarinet and two bassoons, Strauss directs that 'from this point the mounting excitement is to have a suggestion of parody', rather as if he were suggesting that we must not take this love affair too seriously. He underlines this point by musical parody of the love duet from Wagner's *Tristan und Isolde*. No couple can sustain such physical ecstasy for long and as the orchestral texture is thinned, the passion drains from the strings and the tempo slackens as the oboe sings out [5], clarinets, solo viola and solo cello have a touching little subsidiary figure marked 'sighing' (*seufzend*). Theme [5] is often labelled as the leitmotif of 'Love's resignation' or 'Renunciation', but Strauss uses it whenever the Marschallin muses on the passing of her youth and the concomitant loss of a young lover like Octavian. The Introduction ends with a *tranquillo* coda for strings, woodwind and four horns based on the unforgettably tender melody [6] associated with the Marschallin, whom we see in bed with Octavian kneeling beside her as the curtain rises. The cellos' *molto espressivo* version of [1], now tender where it was impetuous, merges into arabesques of birdsong on woodwind. As Octavian sings his praise of his lover — 'Wie du warst! Wie du bist!', *lit.* 'How you were, how you are' — oboe and viola echo his sentiments with [7]. We learn that Octavian's nickname is Quinquin —(Hofmannsthal had discovered that this sobriquet belonged to Count Esterházy von Galantha, who was born in 1715, a little before Octavian). The couple continue their verbal love-making, while Strauss reduces the scoring to chamber-orchestra proportions. When Octavian becomes metaphysical about the meaning of 'you and I', cellos, later joined by violas, quietly hint at the *Tristan* love-motif. When the Marschallin declares her love, [6] floods back. The birdsong is heard again and Octavian runs to the window to draw the curtains across: if he can shut out the day, he says, he can shut out all the other people in the Marschallin's life. An *allegro* [8] begins softly on violins and woodwind and a little bell (triangle) is heard coming nearer. Octavian resents this intrusion. 'No one shall enter, I am master here', he declares, a solo horn quoting, surely ironically, the ardent theme [1] which we first heard from four horns. At whom is this defiance aimed? Only at the Marschallin's little black servant Mohammed, who is bringing her morning chocolate. It is the silver bells sewn to his tunic which we have heard as he approaches. He enters to an enchanting march [9], with a delicate orchestration including tambourine and glockenspiel. The Marschallin — who has been in this situation before — tells Octavian to hide both himself and his sword. When the page has gone she ticks off Octavian for having left his sword in view — hasn't he better manners? He resents this and [1] can be heard in a rather sulky version as he remonstrates with her. But this cloud is dispersed while they have breakfast in waltz tempo [10]. Strauss's scoring for this scene is a pretty example of period pastiche and also a reminder of his early and effective works for wind instruments (the *Serenade* and *Suite*). Tenderness returns, Octavian using the Marschallin's name, Marie Theres', and her pet-name, Bichette, while [4] on the strings accompanies their endearments.

The idyll is broken when Octavian remarks how lucky he is to be with her while the Field Marshal is bear-hunting in the Croatian forest. The Marschallin replies that she dreamt of her husband last night. Octavian's pride is ruffled. 'My dreams are not mine to command,' the Marschallin answers. She had dreamed of hearing the noise of his horses in the courtyard — 'and he was here!' It has reminded her of an occasion when he really had returned unexpectedly. 'But once', ('Einmal'), she begins, but goes no further.

This infuriates Octavian, who demands in vain to know more. All this episode is scored like a scherzo, with rapid ascending flourishes for woodwind and strings as Octavian's temper flares. But now there truly is a disturbance in her dressing-room and the Marschallin is convinced it is her husband arguing with her loyal servants. She tells Octavian to hide. Beneath the agitated strings which tell of her anxiety, an ungainly theme is heard on the bass tuba. As the voice in the anteroom grows louder, she goes to the door to listen. 'That's not my husband's voice', she cries. 'They're saying Herr Baron to him.' And as she calls 'Quinquin, it is someone else', the music, sharing her relief, goes into waltz-time. She identifies 'that foolish loutish voice' as belonging to her cousin Baron Ochs from Lerchenau. Then she remembers that a few days ago (when she was out with Octavian) she was handed a letter. 'That letter came from Ochs and now I have entirely forgotten what it said.' Octavian's [1] is transformed into the waltz theme [11] on oboes and flutes as he reappears dressed as a chambermaid in skirt and short jacket with his hair tied in a handkerchief and ribbon for a cap. 'She' addresses the Marschallin in broad Viennese dialect ('I've not been long in Your Highness's household here') and the Marschallin responds delightedly, 'Quinquin. And only one kiss may I give you. That's for your wages.' ('Du, Schatz! Und nicht einmal mehr als ein Busserl kann ich dir geben.') All this to a lilting waltz, the musical embodiment of a light-hearted masquerade. Every bar of the score up to this point is indicative of Strauss's delight when he received the Act One libretto: 'It'll set itself to music like oil and melted butter: I'm hatching it out already.'[3] He scarcely needed Hofmannsthal's injunction 'Do try and think of an old-fashioned Viennese waltz, sweet and yet saucy, which must pervade the whole of the last act'[4]; waltzes were to pervade the whole score. Censorious English critics rapped Strauss over the knuckles because they thought that his anachronistic use of waltzes was characteristic of his 'carelessness in the matter of style'! Both he and Hofmannsthal by giving Vienna the waltz eighty years early also gave opera a masterstroke of imaginative genius in the creation of an atmosphere.

Baron Ochs (bass) bursts into the room to a loud diminished seventh chord scored for brass, woodwind and strings. Now the music becomes *langsam und gravitätisch* (slow and weighty). He has bumped into Octavian-in-disguise and, ignoring the Marschallin, shows his immediate interest in this 'pretty child' ('hübsches Kind'). It is important to know how Strauss visualised this great character. He wrote in an essay on *Der Rosenkavalier* in 1942[5]: 'Ochs must be a rustic Don Juan beau of about thirty-five, always a nobleman (even if a rather boorish one), who knows how to conduct himself decently in the Marschallin's salon, so that she does not have him thrown out by her servants after five minutes. He is a bounder *inwardly*; but on the surface sufficiently presentable . . . Ochs's first scene in the bedroom must be played with the utmost delicacy and discretion . . . In other words: Viennese comedy not Berlin farce.' All this is summarized in the theme [12] to which he makes his ungainly obeisance — the French bow — to the Marschallin. He is at ease with her, reminding her that he has even called on another princess while that particular lady was having a bath.

In the scene that follows Ochs — in the easy *parlando* recitative style which Strauss began to develop in *Feuersnot* (1900-1) and *Salome* (1904-5), perfected

3. Letter to Hofmannsthal, April 21, 1909.
4. Letter to Strauss, April 24, 1909.
5. R. Strauss: *Recollections and Reflections*, Zurich 1949, London 1953.

Kurt Böhme as Ochs at Covent Garden, 1959. (Covent Garden Archives)

here and in *Ariadne auf Naxos* (1912-16) and used with supreme brilliance in *Intermezzo* (1917-23), *The Silent Woman* (1933-4) and *Capriccio* (1940-1) — is torn between making passes at Octavian and explaining his mission to the Marschallin. For her part, the Marschallin is trying to signal to Octavian to leave and at the same time to make sense of Ochs's narrative (he, naturally, assumes she has read his letter; she has to equivocate). The scoring continues airy and allusive with much use of [13] — a lifetime of acquaintance with the opera will still reveal new subtleties in Strauss's web of motifs. Ochs has come to consult his cousin about his forthcoming marriage to Sophie von Faninal — at the first mention of her a solo cello plays a theme later to be associated with her [14]. She is, he says, fresh from a convent, a mere puppy, healthy, well-washed ('Pudeljung! Gesund! Gewaschen!'), only child of the newly ennobled Faninal who has made a pile of money by supplying the army in the Netherlands. He makes no secret that the money is the principal attraction. While Octavian, whom the Marschallin now addresses as Mariandel, serves Ochs with some of the breakfast chocolate, the Baron asks the favour he has come about. Hofmannsthal invented a Viennese custom by which a silver rose had to be presented to a bride-to-be on behalf of an aristocratic bridegroom by a nobly-born ambassador; Ochs asks her to recommend someone for this task. The Marschallin suggests he should dine with her next day and she will propose a name. But Ochs is not to be dismissed so easily: he also requests the services of her lawyer. The Marschallin sees another chance of getting Octavian out of the room and, as the music goes back into waltz tempo, orders 'her' to see if the lawyer is awaiting her morning levée. A new theme [15] is heard when Ochs refers to Mariandel as 'such a treasure' ('ein solches Goldkind') and stops 'her' exit. At this point the Major-Domo enters to report the arrival of 'the customary riffraff' for the levée. Meanwhile Ochs is trying to 'date' Mariandel for a supper *tête-à-tête* and when she says 'I don't really know if I ought' ('I weiss halt nit, ob i dös derf') bassoons play a waltz theme to be closely associated with Ochs [16]. When the Marschallin laughingly taunts Ochs for flirting even though he is engaged, he launches into a scherzo-like monologue [17] describing how men do not mate by the calendar like animals: there is not a season nor an hour of the day when he is not ready to seduce a woman.

Strauss had reached this point when he told Hofmannsthal: 'My work is flowing along like the Loisach: I am composing everything — neck and crop. I am starting on the levée tomorrow.' This he had already described as 'not easy to put into shape, but I'll manage it all right . . . I'll need very good actors again; the ordinary operatic singers won't do.' He had written the Baron's scene but wanted more lines for it, as well as words for 'a great musical conclusion in the form of a trio . . . I want him to go on bragging of all the things he can do, piling it on thicker and thicker, preferably in a dactylic rhythm . . . overlaid by a duet of the Marschallin, continuing along the theme of "You are going too far! Leave the child alone" . . . And on top of it Octavian, whom I want to let burst into loud laughter . . . Would you add some more text here: the music is all ready and I only need the words for accompaniment and filling in.'[6] This illustrates Strauss's earlier statement that 'for the sake of symphonic unity I must compose the music from the beginning to the end.'

When this trio ends, Ochs asks if he can have Mariandel as servant for his bride — 'she' seems to have 'a drop of good blood' and could be 'a young princess'. He then reveals that his own bastard son acts as his body-servant and will deliver the silver rose to the Marschallin. The Marschallin picks up this clue to explain away Mariandel as Octavian's bastard sister (she realises Ochs is bound to meet Octavian sooner or later) and shows Ochs a medallion of Octavian, suggesting him as the Rose-Bearer. Ochs immediately sees the resemblance to the maid. This dialogue, from Ochs's 'Gad, she could be a

6. Letter to Hofmannsthal, May 16, 1909.

Elizabeth Schwarzkopf (the Marschallin) suggests that the miniature protrait of Octavian is worth Ochs's attention, in Robin Ironside's designs, with Sena Jurinacs as Octavian and Kurt Böhme as Ochs; Covent Garden, 1959. (Covent Garden Archives)

young princess' ('Könnt' eine junge Fürstin sein'), is accompanied by a languid version of the waltz [15] which represents Octavian as Mariandel and, in this wistful setting, perhaps implies that the Marschallin senses danger in employing Octavian as Rose-Bearer. She now orders Mariandel to let in the waiting throng, and the maid escapes at last, slamming the door in Ochs's face.

The levée, based on 'The Contessa's Morning Levée', the fourth engraving in Hogarth's series *Marriage à la Mode*, is one of Strauss's big set pieces in which his gift for character-vignettes, familiar from the tone poems *Till Eulenspiegel, Ein Heldenleben* and *Don Quixote*, enables him to present a busy, colourful scene. On to the stage now come footmen, a lawyer, a chef, a kitchen-boy with menu-book, a milliner, a scholar, an animal-vendor with dogs and monkey, a singer and flautist, a soldier's widow with her three children, and two intriguers, Valzacchi (tenor) and his niece Annina (mezzo-soprano). The three orphaned children implore protection to a lugubrious chant which is interrupted by the various salesmen's cries (the animal-vendor's cry is a quotation from the baby's yells in his bath in the *Symphonia Domestica*, a Garmisch 'in-joke', since the vendor is singing about monkeys and housetrained puppies). The Marschallin introduces her lawyer to Ochs, and

Valzacchi, accompanied by a rapid conspiratorial theme [18] on bass clarinet and muted cellos, tries to interest her in a scandal sheet. She gives the grateful orphans money and a kiss and her hairdresser attends to her coiffure. This scene now becomes a stylized period-piece in minuet tempo, with an elaborate flute part which serves both to illustrate the hairdresser's fingers and to introduce the Tenor's *Di rigori armato il seno* [19], Strauss's testing but affectionate parody of an Italian operatic aria (purloined by Hofmannsthal from the petit-ballet in the fifth act of Molière's *Le bourgeois gentilhomme*).

Ochs has now been joined by his three uncouth servants, one of them his illegitimate son Leopold ('a tall young fellow with a foolish, insolent expression'). He is propounding to the astonished lawyer that his marriage settlement (Morgengabe), instead of being from him to his bride, shall be from her to him and shall consist of his own family estates free of all mortgages. A new theme [20] is signalled by various instruments before it is heard in full on strings and horns. The Tenor begins his second stanza accompanied not only by the flute but by the argument of Ochs and the lawyer. Ochs bangs the table angrily, the Tenor is cut off in mid-aria, and the Marschallin complains that the hairdresser has made her look old. The hairdresser works feverishly to change the style (agitated flutes again) and the Marschallin signs that the levée is ended. While the stage empties, Valzacchi and Annina offer their services to Ochs in a quicksilver *prestissimo* piece of scoring based on [21] and he mentions Mariandel to them. Ochs, to a reprise of [12], introduces Leopold to the Marschallin. The youth gives her the case containing the silver rose. To the music of Sophie's theme [14] and her own love-theme [6], she assures Ochs that Octavian will act as Rose-Bearer.

Now the mood and tenor of the opera change. The Marschallin is left alone for the first time. The wonderful coda contains three superb arias for this woman who, though she appears in only half the opera, dominates it. Although the music he wrote for her in the Introduction shows that Strauss realised her importance from the start, Hofmannsthal did not (like Wagner with Hans Sachs) fully realise it until the libretto was far advanced. Then he wrote[7]: 'She is the central figure for the public, for the women above all, the figure with whom they feel and *move*.' It is important, again, to know how Strauss visualised her — 'a young and beautiful woman of not more than 32 who, when she is in a bad mood, occasionally feels herself an "old hag" compared with 17-year-old Octavian'. In the 18th century 32 was older than it is today, but the practice of making the Marschallin a woman in her fifties is a distortion of the composer's intentions.

Ochs's [12] is now transformed into something like a tragic theme by violins and violas over a plodding bass as the Marschallin muses on the Baron's attitude to his marriage. The orchestral texture is reduced to that of a chamber orchestra as solo strings and clarinet introduce [22], a theme very similar to the opening of *Till Eulenspiegel*, when she remembers how she herself had come from a convent to an arranged marriage. She looks in her mirror, contemplates her old age and how the crowds will point her out as the old Princess. The oboe poignantly quotes [5] as she reflects that this all has to be endured — the difference lies in *how* ('*Wie*') one endures it. And on the word '*Wie*' a bare octave on the harp gives a sharp pang to the strings' gentle chord. Octavian re-enters in riding kit. He senses the Marschallin's changed mood and tries to cheer her up and to protest his love to an orchestral background compounded of their love themes and their earlier discussion of the Field

7. Letter to Strauss, June 6, 1910.

Adele Leigh as Octavian in riding costume. (Covent Garden Archives)

Marshal. She gently rejects Octavian's advances and reflects that nothing will last, that even he will desert her. Now, in a tranquil 6/8, she begins her monologue on the strangeness of time [23], how one is suddenly aware of it, how she sometimes gets up in the night to stop all the clocks (and their soft chimes are magically evoked by celesta and two harps playing harmonics), how her belief in God comforts her. Octavian's response, sensuously tender, is to offer himself as a more accessible substitute for God, but the Marschallin insists that one day he will leave her for a younger and more beautiful woman — and she sings those words, prophetically, to a variation of Sophie's [14]. They argue heatedly but the Marschallin insists it will happen, today or tomorrow ('Heut' oder morgen'), and asks Octavian to leave. In her third and most touching solo, which is the quintessence of nostalgia, based on the themes [5] and [2] and with melting *glissandi* in the strings, she describes how she will go to church, visit her old and ailing Uncle Greifenklau (*lit.* Griffon-claw) and ride in the Prater where Octavian, if he wishes, may join her.

Moved, Octavian leaves. (Strauss knew he had done well here: 'that certain Viennese sentimentality of the parting scene has come off very well. My wife likes it very much', he told his librettist[8].) The orchestra bursts out as the Marschallin panics — she has not even kissed him. She sends her footmen after him but they breathlessly report that they have missed him. In the nostalgic key of E flat, she calls for Mohammed, [9a], and, to the expressive music of [6], orders him to take the silver rose to Octavian. The act ends with her deep in thought as the solo violin and high woodwind play a transfigured version of Octavian's principal motif [1].

Act Two

This act, set in Faninal's palatial home, gave the collaborators much more trouble than Act One. The published Correspondence reveals the fascinating changes which were made. Suffice it to say that Strauss received the libretto to Act Two in June 1909. On July 9 he wrote the first of several detailed criticisms. It lacked 'the necessary clash and climax . . . if Act Two falls flat the opera is lost'. He accepted it up to Ochs's entrance. Thereafter everything that happens was Strauss's idea, including such details as Ochs's neglecting to tip Annina at the end, and he asked Hofmannsthal for 'much more witty and polished' dialogue, adding: 'Don't forget that the audience should also laugh!

8. Letter to Hofmannsthal, May 22, 1909.

Elizabeth Schumann as Sophie, who created the role in Hamburg a few weeks after the Dresden première in 1911, and continued to sing it throughout her career (many times opposite Lehmann at Covent Garden) until 1938.

Tiana Lemnitz as Octavian, 1936. (Covent Garden Archives)

Laugh, not just smile or grin!' Hofmannsthal was not offended. 'I realise myself that for the stage the new version is very much more effective . . . and I am very grateful for your energetic intervention.'

The prelude illustrates, *molto allegro*, the excitement of the preparations for the arrival of the Rose-Bearer [24, 25]. An imposing version of the wedding theme [20] is heard in canon and the prelude ends with [25] followed by a richly scored fanfare for his ambassador [26]. Faninal (baritone) hails this great and holy day and leaves Sophie with her duenna, Marianne Leitmetzerin (soprano). While the duenna reports everything that is happening in the street, Sophie sings [27] of her lonely state, motherless in this solemn hour. But Marianne's description of the Rose-Bearer's procession, the couriers' off-stage calls of Rofrano and the orchestra's recollection of [1] and [26] bring her to an agitated pitch of anticipation. To an emphatic *fortissimo* [26] followed by a fully-scored chord of F sharp major, with a cymbal-clash and rolls of drum and triangle, the doors open to reveal Octavian, a dazzling figure in silver from head to foot and holding out the silver rose. The justly famous and beloved Presentation of the Silver Rose is based on [28] (derived from Sophie's [14]), first heard on the oboe and marked 'very expressively' (*sehr ausdrucksvoll*), with the addition of the unforgettable glittering [28b], scored for 3 flutes, 3 solo violins, celesta and two harps, which is repeated several times throughout the presentation. Octavian diffidently offers the rose. Sophie accepts it, remarks on its scent (from a drop of Persian attar) and, in a soaring ecstatic phrase, describes it as 'like heavenly, not earthly flowers' ('Wie himmlische, nicht irdische, wie Rosen'). For the first time their eyes meet and, very softly, a solo trumpet plays [29], the theme of love-at-first-sight to which they later sing their rapturous duet. Strauss then subtly relaxes the

Valerie Masterson (Sophie) and Josephine Barstow (Octavian) in the ENO production by John Copley.

tension into a slightly formal, almost embarrassed conversation (*animato grazioso*) between the two young people, supervised by the duenna. Sophie tells Octavian she knows his age and all his names [30], and she even knows that his close friends call him Quinquin. It is another of those moments of repose in which the opera abounds.

But now Ochs and his disreputable retinue are introduced by Faninal, to a march-like version of [25]. Ochs inspects Sophie as if she were horse-flesh, to Octavian's fury and Sophie's disgust. He remarks on Octavian's likeness to 'a certain someone' and reveals the existence of 'a little bastard sister', before he tries to woo Sophie on his knee. Faninal is complacently delighted by what he sees, Octavian enraged. Ochs continues to tease Sophie, who asks 'What are you to me?'. Och's obvious reply — that she will discover the answer overnight — leads him to quote his favourite song and the line (*lit.*) 'with me no night will be too long' ('Mit mir keine Nacht dir zu lang'). This is the most famous tune in the opera [31, 32]. It was written as a parody of Johann Strauss but has equalled the real thing in the public's affections. (Undoubtedly this is some of the music Strauss wrote in advance of the libretto, since tune and words do not fit each other all that well.) Ochs, revelling in what he calls 'the luck of the Lerchenaus' [33], is then taken by Faninal to attend to legal formalities, but before he goes invites Octavian to take what liberties he likes with the 'young unbroken filly'.

Left together (except for the duenna) Sophie appeals for Octavian's help [34]. There is a sudden uproar as Ochs's men chase Faninal's maids through the room, and the duenna leaves to aid the Major-Domo. Now the lovers are alone. They enjoy their first kiss and their duet [35] is a tender affair, Strauss having obeyed Hofmannsthal's injunction to avoid 'a Wagnerian kind of erotic screaming'. On its last note Valzacchi and Annina, who have tiptoed in, seize them and call for Ochs. Octavian decides, rather ineffectually, to tell the Baron of Sophie's dislike but Ochs contemptuously mocks him. When the Baron tries to steer Sophie into the room where the lawyer is waiting, Octavian bars their way, flings insults at the Baron and draws his sword. Ochs summons his followers with a piercing whistle, but the sight of the sword deters them. In a scuffle Ochs brushes its point and yells 'Murder'. A farcical ensemble (all Strauss's idea) follows, in which Ochs is tended, most incompetently, by his retinue and a doctor; Faninal's servants fill the stage wondering what has happened, while Annina harangues them, saying that Octavian and Sophie were already secretly engaged; the duenna helps to tend Ochs; and Faninal toadies to Ochs (and, feeling very sorry for himself, rounds on his daughter, telling her she has the choice of marriage to Ochs's corpse if necessary or a convent for life). Sophie is now all defiance, and Octavian leaves with a whispered word to Valzacchi and Annina.

Faninal's posturings irritate Ochs, who asks for some wine in order to get rid of him. This ensemble is a masterly example of Strauss's ability to keep the top spinning while the stage action is predominant. Ochs, his arm now in a sling, bemoans his fate in Vienna and curses Octavian who has caused his arm to hurt when he tries to drink. (His monologue was inspired by Falstaff's 'Mondo ladro' in Verdi's opera when the Fat Knight has climbed dripping from the Thames and warms himself with wine.) A gentler version of [12], however, tells us that Ochs is feeling better and the 'luck of the Lerchenaus' theme [33] (and other waltzes [31]) accompanies his amusement at the memory of Sophie's tantrums. Annina now comes in with a letter, which Ochs asks her to read aloud. It is from Mariandel — now we know what Octavian was saying to the conspirators before he left — suggesting a meeting next evening and awaiting an answer. Ochs is overjoyed. Ignoring Annina's importuning for a tip, he tells her to set up a writing-table and he will dictate his reply. The orchestra plays a sumptuous version of [31] and Ochs contentedly sings the last lines, ending on a low E held for six bars. Strauss wrote to Hofmannsthal on September 18, 1909: 'The final conclusion of Act Two is now all composed and, I believe, has turned out a first-class hit. "I am satisfied with myself".'

Act Three

Hofmannsthal wrote to Strauss on September 20, 1909: 'As soon as I have got my comedy out of the way, I shall tackle Act Three . . . It must become the best of all, gay and full of feeling, and ought, in the character of the Marschallin, to touch once again the more sublime chords of tenderness.' Some time early in 1910 the libretto of the first part of the act reached Strauss. But he wanted it all. On April 23 he wrote, 'I am in Garmisch and am in agonies waiting for Act Three!'. Hofmannsthal's reply four days later promised more but added: 'Only the very end, the trio-duet, which needs much subtlety and yet great sweetness, has had to be put off until now when I am feeling better and more in the mood . . . I did so want to write this last scene, a matter of only three or four pages, out in the garden.' By May 2, Strauss had started to compose Act Three. It is interesting to note that as early as June 26, 1909, Strauss told his librettist that 'for the end of Act Three, the softly-fading duet of Sophie and Octavian, I have a very pretty tune'. He then asked for 12 to 16 lines in a particular rhythm. Nearly a year later, when Hofmannsthal came to write the words of the duet, he told Strauss he was 'obviously very much tied down by the metre scheme which you presented for me, but in the end I found it rather agreeable to be bound in this way to a given tune since I felt in this something Mozartian . . . ' At this stage the intention was still to call the opera *Ochs von Lerchenau*. Not until June 10, 1910 did the title *Rosenkavalier* occur in the correspondence. One further quotation illustrates the delight and care with which this masterpiece was created. Hofmannsthal to Strauss, May 4, 1910: 'I would have found the end long ago but for the appalling weather . . . The end must be *very* good, or it will be no good at all. It must be psychologically convincing and at the same time tender, the words must be charming and easy to sing, it must be properly split up into conversation and again into numbers, it must provide a happy ending for the young people and yet not make one too uncomfortable about the Marschallin. In short, it must be done with zest and joy, and so I must sit in the garden and have sun, not icy rainstorms.'

The third act opens with a long orchestral Introduction and Pantomime, *vivace possibile*. It is a fugato based on the conspirators' themes [18] and [21] and their derivatives, and it obviously describes conspiratorial activities. Octavian's [1] is presented in mercurial shape, Ochs's [25] mockingly. The scoring is light-fingered. When the first bars are repeated, the curtain rises on a private room in an inn in a disreputable suburb of Vienna. Annina is disguised in mourning and Valzacchi is adjusting her veil. Octavian, in his Mariandel disguise but wearing riding boots beneath his skirt, makes a brief appearance. He throws a purse to Valzacchi. Valzacchi shows five men to hiding-places under trap-doors, and behind fake windows and sliding panels. He claps his hands and they rehearse their 'materialisations' and 'disappearances' [36]. A waiter and a boy light candles (woodwind trills) and arrange the dining table. So far not a word has been sung, while the orchestra has played a string of waltzes. We hear much of Ochs's [16] and of Octavian-as-Mariandel's [11]. As the candles are lit, an off-stage orchestra begins to play more waltzes, one of which is [16], but the others — [37], [38], associated with the waiters, and [39] — are new[9]. Strauss here shows himself the equal of Johann Strauss in *Die Fledermaus*. Indeed, he himself wrote in 1925: 'How could I have written the *Rosenkavalier* waltzes without the example of the merry genius of Vienna?'

Ochs, his arm still in a sling, enters with Mariandel. He extinguishes the candles, complains about the music, and says he does not need the waiters, because his Leopold will serve the meal. Alone with Mariandel at last, he pours some wine for her, which she refuses to the languid strain of [40]. She says she wants to leave and, 'mistaking' a curtained alcove for an exit, discloses a bed. 'Who's it for?' 'You'll know in good time', Ochs replies[10]. As he pulls Mariandel towards him, her resemblance to 'that blasted boy' disturbs him, and an eruption in the brass disturbs the flow of waltzes [41, 42]. One of the trap-door apparitions [36] jumps the gun and terrifies Ochs. Mariandel (who has signalled to the man to close his door) pacifies the Baron. The off-stage band now strikes up with [31] in a highly schmaltzy version, which to Ochs's ill-concealed irritation, reduces Mariandel to maudlin tears [43]. He removes his wig, revealing a bald scalp, and grapples with Mariandel's bodice. This prompts Octavian to signal for pandemonium to break loose on stage and in the orchestra. The apparitions appear, one of them takes the wig, while another — the disguised Annina — threatens Ochs and then claims histrionically that he is her husband. Children dance around him screaming 'Papa!'. Ochs opens the window and calls for the police. The Police Commissar (bass baritone) questions Ochs and the landlord. Although Ochs says Valzacchi will vouch for him, the Italian, firmly in Octavian's pay, knows nothing, of course. Leopold, concerned at the way things are going, runs out. He has gone, as we shall discover, to fetch the Marschallin — this was Strauss's explanation for the arrival of this high-born lady in such an unlikely place. Yes, it is a creaky part of the plot but, by now, who cares? At the moment Ochs tells the Commissar that Mariandel is his fiancée, Sophie von Faninal, in walks Faninal (summoned by Valzacchi on Octavian's instructions, but thinking he has been called by Ochs). Ochs tries to disown Faninal. The orchestra is a web of thematic fragments which sustain the mood during the tomfoolery. Strauss found this part of the plot 'rather heavy going for a musician', and sometimes it sounds it.

When the Commissar asks Faninal if Mariandel is his daughter, as Ochs has said, Faninal sends for Sophie, who is sitting outside in the sedan. Her entry restores some dignity to the scene and begins the stretch of magnificent music with which Strauss achieved the opera's emotional crisis. A splendid new version for full orchestra of one of her themes announces her arrival [44], accompanied (when they are not cut, as they often are) by a chorus of onlookers muttering 'The bride — oh what a sore disgrace!'. Faninal indicates Annina and the children to her as Ochs's wife and children and then collapses.

9. The instrumentation of the off-stage band is: 2 flutes, oboe, 1 clarinet in C, 2 clarinets in B, 2 bassoons, 2 horns, 1 trumpet, 1 side-drum, 1 harmonium, 1 piano, violins, violas, cellos, double-basses.

10. In the original 1913 English translation by Alfred Kalisch, there was no mention of the bed. This opera fell foul of the censors in Berlin in 1911, when many lines (especially in Ochs's Act One monologue) were bowdlerised, and until quite recently the Marschallin was never seen in bed on stage.

She helps him to an anteroom. Meanwhile, Ochs has found his wig and begins to feel more like his old self. He tells the Commissar that he'll pay the bill and drive Mariandel home; but the Commissar has more questions for him. The music stops and Octavian asks to make a statement where Ochs cannot hear him. He retires to the alcove, and, as Ochs assures the constables that he has no idea who Annina is, Octavian tosses Mariandel's undergarments to the Commissar (to a 6/8 version of [43]). The excitement mounts until the landlord announces the arrival of the Marschallin.

This great theatrical moment is the fulcrum of the plot, as Hofmannsthal intended it to be. Strauss wrote to him[11]: 'The Marschallin's entrance and the ensuing scene must be the focal point of the action and the suspense, and must be highly concentrated. When the Baron and the whole crowd are gone, then everything can gradually dissolve into a lyrical mood and return to soft outlines.' Hofmannsthal wrote[12] interestingly about his characters' personalities: 'Sophie is a very pretty girl, but she is also a very ordinary girl like dozens of others — this is the whole point of the story; true charm of speech, indeed the stronger charm of personality is all with the Marschallin. Just the fact that, in this criss-cross double adventure, Quinquin falls for the *very first* little girl to turn up, that is the point, that is what unites the whole and holds together the two actions. The Marschallin remains the dominant female figure, between Ochs and Quinquin — Sophie always stands one step below these chief characters . . . Even the musical, conceptual unity of the whole opera would suffer if the personality of the Marschallin were to be deprived of her full stature . . . ' Strauss scarcely needed this lesson in the creation of operatic women. Already in *Salome* and *Elektra*, he had shown his insight into feminine psychology, and after *Der Rosenkavalier* he was to add further portraits to this gallery, Zerbinetta and Ariadne in *Ariadne auf Naxos*, the Empress and the Dyer's Wife in *Die Frau ohne Schatten*, his own wife Pauline in *Intermezzo*, the charming Arabella, the humanised mythological characters Helen, Daphne and Danae, and (nearest of all to the Marschallin) the Countess in his

11. Letter to Hofmannsthal, May 20, 1910.
12. Letter to Strauss, July 12, 1910.

Viorica Ursuleac as the Marschallin.
(Covent Garden Archives)

wonderful last opera *Capriccio*. Many would argue that the Marschallin remains his greatest creation. He certainly was in no doubt how to project her in the closing pages of the opera. As late as September 10, 1910 Hofmannsthal had misgivings about the ending and sent Strauss a shortened version. Strauss's reply was to the point: 'That it sounds a bit flat in reading is obvious. But it is at the conclusion that a musician, if he has any ideas at all, can achieve his best and supreme effects — so you may safely leave this for me to judge.' How right he was can now be heard.

The Marschallin is followed by little Mohammed carrying her train. A sumptuous and stately version of [5] is played on high woodwind and high strings — one can almost hear the sweep of her dress — and on the basset-horn, bassoons and cellos is a quickened version of [1] as Octavian puts his head between the curtains of the alcove to ask what brings her here. The Marschallin ignores him while she recognises the Commissar as having been her husband's orderly. Ochs, who signals to Leopold his pleasure at the success of his 'rescue' mission, is convinced the Marschallin has come to extricate him and gestures to Octavian (still Mariandel to him) to stay in the alcove, but when he turns his back Octavian, now in male attire, steps out. Sophie returns, does not see the Marschallin, and tells Ochs she has a message from Faninal. That, says Octavian to the Marschallin, is the girl for whose sake . . . he needs to say no more. 'Who she is I can surely guess. She has great charm,' the Marschallin replies icily, for the only time in the opera addressing Octavian as Rofrano. (Among the delights of Hofmannsthal's libretto are the subtleties of language and etiquette, some of them lost in translation, and the use of dialect for Ochs and Mariandel.) Sophie shows herself something of a spitfire, telling Ochs that Faninal warns him not to come within a hundred paces of his house, or else. She here adopts the aristocratic third-person style of address. Theme [24], Faninal's principal motif, crackles through the orchestra during this outburst.

When Ochs tries to push past Sophie into the room where Faninal is resting, the Marschallin orders him to put a good face on the situation and to leave with dignity. Parts of [12] and [13] are heard on violins, violas and woodwind as Ochs shows stupefaction. It has all been a farce, you see, the Marschallin tells the Commissar, a phrase which is echoed emptily by the shocked Sophie. To the throb of horns and basses, the Marschallin tells Octavian to make Ochs see sense. Octavian's relish in this — [1] and [16] — is obvious. When the Marschallin incautiously interjects that she is displeased with men in general at the moment [5], Ochs at last weighs up the situation between Octavian and the Marschallin and, as the tender love-theme [6] returns in splendour, says he does not know what he ought to think. 'You will just refrain from thinking,' is the Marschallin's edict. Many Ochs themes recur as he believes he has triumphed over the Marschallin. He will forget everything and make it up with Faninal. With [20], the theme of the wedding preparations, in full sail in the orchestra, the Marschallin imperiously informs him that everything — including his engagement — is finished. At last, to a falling cadence similar to that in *Till Eulenspiegel* which marks the end of the rogue's escapades, Ochs faces reality. So does Sophie, who believes her love for Octavian must be finished too, and she repeats the Marschallin's 'Ist halt vorbei' (*lit.* 'Is simply finished') to a pathetic reminiscence of the rapturous phrase with which she had received the silver rose. The Marschallin, whose thoughts are precisely similar where Octavian is concerned, sings her phrase to [5]. These musings merge into the orchestra's quiet recapitulation of the act's Introduction. To its ghostly flickering, all the conspirators enter, the landlord presenting the bill, the children screaming 'Papa'. They advance on Ochs, who calls out 'Leupold, wir gehn!' ('We go'). At this the waltzes return, first [33] as Annina and Valzacchi taunt him with 'the luck of the Lerchenaus' theme [31], the dinner waltz [37] and, on horns, the theme with which in Act One the Marschallin expressed her relief that her husband had not returned. Against this kaleidoscope of sound [41], the bills are presented, the children yell, and Ochs and Leopold finally escape, chased by the crowd.

The waltz tempo of [41] continues when the Marschallin, Octavian and Sophie are left together. The masquerade really is over, and the listener will sense Strauss rising to the challenge of a deeper theme. Octavian does not know which woman to console but the Marschallin, taut and controlled, sends him to Sophie. To a simple waltz [45], Octavian asks Sophie for a tender greeting. The Marschallin's renunciation theme [5] is merged into [45]; and there is another reminiscence from Act One as she recalls her words 'Heut' oder morgen' ('Today or tomorrow') while she watches Octavian reiterate his love to Sophie. In this ensemble, [45] combines with the Act One love-duet in a passionate climax. It is Sophie now who is perceptive, and sends Octavian to the distressed Marschallin, saying she must go to her father. When Octavian orders her to stay, the Marschallin approaches Sophie and, with [5] *con moto grazioso* on the first violins, asks if she already loves Octavian so much. The embarrassed girl, turning into a nervous chatterbox, ascribes her pale cheeks to the shock she has had over her father. The Marschallin, worldly-wise and kindly, stops her prattle. She knows the cure for Faninal's ills; she will invite him to drive home with her in her carriage, along with Sophie herself and Octavian.

The young lovers are deeply moved. The Trio that follows is not only the supreme moment of the opera but one of the supreme moments of all opera, comparable with the Quintet in Wagner's *The Mastersingers of Nuremberg* and incomparable as an example of writing for three soprano voices. Octavian softly sings 'Marie Theres'' while the orchestra holds a long chord, except for a solo trumpet which quietly plays [5]. Then, *moderato e molto cantabile*, the Marschallin sings the first high, floating phrase [46]. This melody is in fact just a transfiguration of Mariandel's *'Nein, nein'* theme [40] from the supper-scene! Into the glowing, rich and immensely intricate vocal texture, the themes of [5] and [1] are interwoven. Each of the three soliloquises: Octavian about his love for Sophie; Sophie about the Marschallin and, at the end, as she looks into Octavian's eyes, about her own love; and the Marschallin about her renunciation of Octavian. The voices soar to a climax, and there is a glorious orchestral peroration based on [5], with Octavian's [1] on cellos and bassoons, and the silver rose music [28a and b] in the woodwind. With the enigmatic phrase 'In Gottes Namen' that suggests both her resignation and her blessing, the Marschallin quietly leaves.

The music of the Presentation of the Rose returns as Sophie and Octavian move closer to each other. Over a high soft tremolo, Sophie's [14] is repeated several times by oboe and flute while [1] spreads over the whole orchestra. They embrace and begin the chaste duet [47] which so perfectly complements the ardour of the Trio. (It may be compared with the Purcellian simplicity of the Fenton-Nannetta duet in Verdi's *Falstaff*.) To a recapitulation of the music with which she sent Octavian from her at the end of Act One, the Marschallin now re-enters with Faninal. 'Sind halt aso, die jungen Leut' (*lit.* 'That's how they are, the young folk'), Faninal sings benevolently. The Marschallin replies

'Ja, Ja' — and to those two notes the memorable interpreters of this rôle impart a whole world of experience, the strings at their sweetest telling us of the Marschallin's self-sacrifice. Alone again, Sophie and Octavian resume their duet, with each phrase underlined by the glittering [28b]. During an embrace Sophie drops her handkerchief. Their last words are sung to [29], with [28b] chiming out as they kiss and run out hand-in-hand. The stage is empty, and Strauss devises a codetta akin to the delicate epilogue of *Till Eulenspiegel*. We hear Mohammed's tinkling bells [9]. The Marschallin has sent him back. Candle in hand he searches, finds the handkerchief and, waving it triumphantly, runs off to the accompaniment of brilliant, happy, final chords.

So ends an opera which, in its eighty years of existence, has already created its own mythology of interpreters of the various rôles, a mythology which the gramophone converts into reality for the listeners of today and tomorrow. Everything about it seems to have been blessed with the certainty of success. 'I pray that you are content — for myself I must say I so enjoyed working on this piece that it almost saddens me to have to write "Curtain" ', Hofmannsthal wrote to Strauss in 1910. And, when he was over eighty and had had many more triumphs, Richard Strauss was content to identify himself with the words, 'I am the composer of *Der Rosenkavalier*'.

Extracts from the Correspondence between Strauss and Hofmannsthal are quoted by kind permission of Cambridge University Press, publishers of the English translation by Hanns Hammelmann and Ewald Osers.

Hugo von Hofmannsthal, an oil painting on wood, by Hans Schlesinger
(Courtesy of Octavian von Hofmannsthal)

Hugo von Hofmannsthal — Man of Letters

Peter Branscombe

Hugo von Hofmannsthal crammed a bewildering variety of activities into a comparatively short life. By the beginning of the last decade of the nineteenth century, when he was still in his mid teens, he was recognized as one of the most brilliant poetic talents in Vienna, already admitted to the circle around Hermann Bahr, Schnitzler (for whose *Anatol* he wrote the verse prologue) and Richard Beer-Hoffmann. He produced a quantity of lyric verse of a delicacy of perception and power of imagery that can perhaps be paralleled only by Rimbaud's rather earlier yet equally precocious poetry. But at the same time he was beginning to write a series of verse plays — plays for reading rather than for staging — such as *Gestern (Yesterday)*, *Der Tod des Tizian (The Death of Titian)* and *Der Tor und der Tod (The Fool and Death)*; before the decade was out there were nearly a dozen of them, including scenarios which were to become ballets with the music of Egon Wellesz (*Achilles auf Skyros*) and Zemlinsky (*Der Triumph der Zeit, The Triumph of Time* — though as composed it was named *Das gläserne Herz, The Heart of Glass*). The titles suggest the range of his interests at that time, just as the lyric poems indicated the uncanny insight he had acquired into the minds of people totally outside his own experience — a state of preternaturally mature understanding which he called *Praeexistenz* (literally 'pre-existence', referring to knowledge which must be assumed to have been acquired in a previous existence). The rich vein of poetic inspiration which he mined during the '90s ran out quite suddenly in the earliest years of the new century, shortly after he graduated Dr. phil. at Vienna with a thesis on linguistic usage in the group of sixteenth-century French poets known as the Pléiade.

It was at this stage in his career — 1900, and he was 26 — that he first came into contact with Richard Strauss. Initially, there can be little doubt, Hofmannsthal looked upon a possible collaboration with Germany's foremost musician as a solution to his own creative problems. However, for the moment Strauss declined the ballet-scenario *The Triumph of Time* which Hofmannsthal offered him, and their partnership did not begin until a few years later. Hofmannsthal sought to come to terms with his own problems of creativity and communication by adapting great works from the past, from various cultures. More intimately, he chose the extraordinary form of a fictitious letter from Lord Chandos to Francis Bacon (*Ein Brief — A Letter*) to express his own perception that words could no longer adequately convey a writer's meaning. Though this crisis was of comparatively short duration, the difficulties of communication were to remain an abiding concern of Hofmannsthal's, as they were at different times for such contrasting contemporaries as Wittgenstein, Kafka and Schoenberg.

For the time being, however, he sought a solution to his artistic problems in the translation and adaptation of foreign dramatists, including Otway in *Das gerettete Venedig (Venice Preserved)*, and Sophocles in *Ödipus und die Sphinx* and *König Ödipus*. In 1906 his collaboration with Strauss began, after the composer had reacted enthusiastically to the Berlin production of Hofmannsthal's version of *Elektra* (in its original form as a spoken play). The poet was asked to make certain changes and cuts for Strauss's purposes — and the most productive partnership in the history of opera was born.

Harold Barrett as the Marschallin's page in the first Covent Garden production, 1913. He later became a Stage Manager at the Royal Opera House. (Covent Garden Archives)

Although there is no precise dividing-line between his plays and his librettos, and indeed prose works and poems too as far as subject-matter is concerned, Hofmannsthal does tend to concentrate the attention in his opera-books on those aspects of femininity and of love which held a particular appeal for Strauss as well as for himself. The librettos explore the relationship between man and woman on various levels, and in two main thematic areas (the myth, and the sentimental comedy of manners). Even *Elektra* — which was not so much a collaboration between a librettist and a composer as the setting of an already-existing play — for all its insistence on the theme of vengeance, touches on the subject of love and child-bearing as the ideal of the gentle Chrysothemis. In the librettos after *Der Rosenkavalier* Hofmannsthal depicts love in a variety of ways. *Ariadne* reveals in the contrast between Ariadne and Zerbinetta, and the attraction between Ariadne and Bacchus, stylized forms of conventional operatic love. *Die Frau ohne Schatten* shows two pairs of lovers whose relationships are foundering on limited understanding — relationships that can only be made meaningful through self-sacrifice. Love in *Die ägyptische Helena* is the spiritual resilience which is capable of surviving passing infatuation and the temptations of deception, and wins through to trust. *Arabella*, the last libretto Hofmannsthal lived to write (but did not live to

34

revise and polish), shows up the incomplete nature of 'ordinary' human love when it is set against the perfect trust and generosity of spirit which Arabella and Mandryka finally achieve.

All these aspects of love are given vitality, directness and charm by Hofmannsthal's ability to fuse concept with language and gesture. Running through the librettos is, for instance, water-imagery. Chrysothemis uses the analogy of pregnant women struggling to bear water-pots from the well; water is the element over which Bacchus, greeted as if he were Charon, comes to bring not death but renewed life and love to Ariadne; in *Die Frau ohne Schatten* water plays an unusually large role, both in points of detail and in the final tableau, with a golden stream cascading before the re-united couples as promise of fruitfulness; *Arabella* takes from Slav folksong the motif of the glass of pure water given to her future husband by the bride.

Another recurrent theme connected with love is the creation of a meaningful family unit (for Hofmannsthal increasingly a vital concern in the chaotic years of European political and social disintegration). It is the message of the beautiful comedy *Der Schwierige (The Difficult Man)*, as it is of the roughly contemporaneous *Frau ohne Schatten*. The decision of Hans-Karl, the 'difficult man' of the play's title, virtually to retire from society and remove to his estate with Helene can be viewed as escapism; yet in the circumstances of post-war Austria, Hofmannsthal was as convinced as Stifter had been after the 1848 Revolution that the future of society at large was dependent on the unit of the family. Lest the accusation that the poet was advocating escapism should nevertheless stick, it should be pointed out that in his final play, *Der Turm (The Tower)*, he probed the disquieting political realities of the '20s, set in a central European mythical-historical context. Here for the last time he reworked a powerful foreign work — Calderón's *La vida es sueño (Life is a Dream)* — so as to cast fresh light on the recurrent problems of sifting permanent from transient values, of fostering the resilient, self-sacrificing spirit of true humanity in a world heavy with corruption.

One may also see Hofmannsthal's concern for international understanding, for the need to transmit the basic values of civilization, in his determined work with Max Reinhardt and others after the First World War to establish the Salzburg Festival as a meeting-place for artists and art-lovers at which works of eminence from past and present should be given in exemplary performances, and by which better understanding between nations should be encouraged. This principle underlies many of his adaptations — *Jedermann* (his version of the old English morality play of *Everyman*) before the War, after the War *Das grosse Salzburger Welttheater (The Great Salzburg Theatre of the World)*. The latter, though less inextricably a part of the Salzburg Festival than *Jedermann*, is the more ambitious play, with its parabolic reflection of the dark forces at work in Europe, and its emphasis on individual responsibility if chaos is to be averted.

From the conscious and admitted adaptations it is fascinating to turn to the hidden literary borrowings, more or less conscious memories of his passionate and voracious reading in several languages; antecedents of the most varied kind can be found for a vast number of tiny details in his writings. Yet these borrowings are so creative, his use of them so subtle, that the accusation that he was a kleptomaniac has only the most superficial application. Hofmannsthal was equally likely to draw his inspiration from a novel or a folksong, a play or a myth, a volume of memoirs or a history book; on occasion he adapted a scene from a painting (Hogarth's 'Levée' in *Rosenkavalier*, Act One), or even modelled a character on an acquaintance (Strauss's wife was the prototype for the Empress in *Die Frau ohne Schatten*). The immediacy of his character-depiction clearly owes much to his loving compilation of detail; even minor characters come vividly to life.

Hofmannsthal's concern with the problem of communication is of crucial importance throughout his life, and may be studied in such disparate and chronologically widely separated works as the early lyric poem, *Die Beiden, Der Schwierige* (for instance in the scene in which Hans-Karl tries to propose marriage), and the preface to the volume of essays *Wert und Ehre deutscher Sprache* (literally, 'Worth and Honour of the German Language') two years before his death, in which he hoped by pointing to treasures from Germany's literary past to help young people come to a proper understanding of the need to preserve the spirit of the German language. Problems of communication — of winning through to a mature understanding of the nature of another person — also play an important part within the librettos: in *Elektra* it is the relationship between the protagonist and her brother and sister; in *Der Rosenkavalier* between Octavian and the Marschallin, Octavian and Sophie; in *Ariadne* the focus is on Ariadne and Bacchus, but also on artist and public, artist and artist. *Die Frau ohne Schatten* focuses attention on the lack of insight between the two couples, in *Die ägyptische Helen* the concern is for the relationship between the long-separated husband and wife, and in *Arabella* it is for the engaged couple who must rise above misunderstandings.

Not the least interesting aspect of the Hofmannsthal-Strauss partnership is the choice of subjects they finally made and followed through to successful conclusion, and the subjects proposed and temporarily pursued by the one, but rejected by the other. It is curious to think we might have had a Hofmannsthal-Strauss *Semiramis*, odder still to think what a Hofmannsthal-Strauss *Intermezzo* might have been like. Strauss also tried to wheedle out of the poet a libretto on a French Revolution subject, or something lurid from the Italian Renaissance. To these and similar requests Hofmannsthal could only just keep a note of censure from the wording of his refusal. Nor was Strauss always keen to follow Hofmannsthal in his inclinations, *Christinas Heimreise*, a play based on an incident from Casanova's life being one example, and a proposed ballet on the subject of Orestes and the Furies another. The fact that there was tension and disagreement in the working relationship was surely to its advantage — neither of the collaborators was able or indeed willing entirely to submerge his own artistic personality in the interests of the other. Each made sacrifices, but it was Hofmannsthal, the more delicate of the partners, who was better able — thanks not least to his intellectual toughness and resilience — to maintain his own independent creative development during the years of their co-operation, as the impressive list of works written for his own rather than Strauss's purposes indicates.

In the letter he wrote to congratulate Strauss on his sixtieth birthday, in June 1924, Hofmannsthal remarked that it seemed to him to be 'something great and also necessary in my life that you approached me, eighteen years ago now, with your wishes and needs. It was pre-ordained that I am able to fulfil this wish — within the limitations of my talents — and that this fulfilment should in turn satisfy an inner need in me . . . You have rewarded me as far as one artist can reward another . . . '. A further reward, which Hofmannsthal did not live to see, is that his example of providing a corpus of dignified, poetic librettos has helped contemporaries and successors of such varied outlooks as Brecht, Cocteau, Busoni, E.M. Forster, Ingeborg Bachmann, Christopher Fry, Gertrude Stein, Auden and Kallman (whose *Elegy for Young Lovers* is dedicated to Hofmannsthal's memory) to perceive the worth of operatic collaboration.

Frieda Hempel as the Marschallin and Margaret Ober as Octavian in the American première at the Met., December 9, 1913.

*Left. The first performance:
Eva von der Osten (Octavian)
and Margarethe Siems (the
Marschallin) in the 1911
Dresden production.*

*Below. The same scene at
Covent Garden in 1975 with
Brigitte Fassbaender
(Octavian) and Gwyneth
Jones (the Marschallin), in
Visconti's production.
(photo: Donald Southern)*

Thematic Guide

Many of the themes from the opera have been identified in the articles by numbers in square brackets, which refer to the themes set out on these pages. The themes are also identified by the numbers in brackets at the corresponding points in the libretto, so that the words can be related to the musical themes.

[7]

A tempo mosso

[8]

Allegro

[9a]

[9b]

[10]

Tempo di Waltz

[11]

Vivo

[12]

Pesante

[13] Commodo

[14]

[15] Con moto

[16] Tempo di Waltz

[17] OCHS

Presto

Is that a - ny rea - son to live like a monk?
Macht das ei - nem leh - men E - sel aus mir?

[18] Presto

[19] THE ITALIAN TENOR

Un poco sostenuto

Di ri - go - ri ar - ma - to il se - no

41

[20]

Allegro non troppo

[21]

Vivace possibile

[22]

Con moto

[23] **MARSCHALLIN**

Piu tranquillo

For   time,   how strange - ly,   goes   its   own   way
Die   Zeit,   die   ist   ein   son - der - bar   Ding.

[24]

Molto allegro

[25]

Moderato

[26]

[27] SOPHIE

On this most joy - ful day I praise thee my ma - ker
In die - ser fei - er - li - chen Stun - de der Prü - fung

[28a]

Piuttosto lento

[28b]

[29] SOPHIE

Where have I been be - fore _____ and felt such rap - ture?
Wo war ich schon ein - mal _____ und war so se - lig?

[30] SOPHIE

Animato grazioso

I know you ve - ry well, mon cou - sin!
Ich kenn' Ihn schon recht wohl, mon cou - sin!

[31]

Tempo di Waltz tranquillo

[32]

43

[33] *The Luck of the Lerchenaus*

Waltz mosso

[34] SOPHIE

Andante mosso

My trust is in your kind - ness _____ mon cou - sin,
Zu Ihm hätt' ich ein Zu - traum, _____ mon cou - sin,

[35] OCTAVIAN

Cantabile

With eyes all veiled by your tears you're ask - ing my aid,_
Mit Ih - ren Au - gen voll Trä - nen kommt Sie zu mir,_

[36]

[37]

Tempo di Waltz *con anima*

[38]

Tempo di Valse
con spirito

44

[39]

Molto animato

[40] OCTAVIAN

Un poco languido

No, no,   let be   No wine   for   me.
Nein, nein,   nein, nein   I trink   kein Wein.

[41]

Tempo di Waltz   con grazia

[42]

Waltz un poco commodo

[43] OCTAVIAN

Moderato assai

'Tis all one,   'tis   all   one,
Es is ja   eh alls eins,

45

[44]

Molto allegro sempre

[45] **OCTAVIAN**

Moderato

Eh bien, —— have you no friend - ly word for me?
Eh bien, —— hat Sie kein freund - lich Wort für mich?

[46] **MARSCHALLIN** *(Trio)*

Moderato e molto cantabile

I —— made a vow to love ————— him right - ly
Hab' —— mir's ge - lobt, ihn lieb ————— zu ha - ben

[47] **SOPHIE, OCTAVIAN**

Andante tranquillo

Am I dream- ing that here we stand, one in happ - i -ness and
s.
Ist ein traum kann nicht wirk- lich sein, dass wir zwei bei - ei

Bliss too deep to un - der - stand one in happ - i -ness and
o.
Spür mich dich, spür' nur dich, al - lein und dass wir - bei - ein -

hand in hand,
- an - der sein,

hand in hand!
an - der sein!

46

Der Rosenkavalier
The Rose-Bearer

Comedy for Music in Three Acts

by Hugo von Hofmannsthal
Music by Richard Strauss Op. 59
English version by Alfred Kalisch

Der Rosenkavalier was first performed in Dresden on January 26, 1911. The first performance in Britain was given at Covent Garden on January 29, 1913, and in the United States in New York on December 9 of the same year. There was a production in English by Sadler's Wells Opera at Sadler's Wells on March 8, 1939, and another by English National Opera at the London Coliseum on January 29, 1975.

A Note on the Libretto

The German text given here is based on three sources. The copyright in the piano score prepared by Otto Singer is dated 1911 and 1913, renewed in 1939 by Fürstner Ltd, and assigned in 1943 to Boosey and Hawkes. This text is what is usually reprinted to accompany recordings because it is what is most often sung. It does not, however, exactly match the text in the full score which was published in 1939 with a note giving the authority of Clemens Krauss that 'it is to be taken as authentic'. Stewart Spencer has pointed out that even this full score contains some obvious mistakes. In neither score do we find the idiosyncratic spelling and punctuation of Hofmannsthal's libretto, as published in the 1986 critical edition by Hoffmann and Schuh, which may be taken to represent what Hofmannsthal intended for reading. Even allowing for differences of presentation, that text differs from the scores by including passages which were not set to music, and others where Strauss demanded extra lines which Hofmannsthal did not incorporate into the main body of his libretto.

We have chosen to follow the text of the 1939 full score, on the basis of Clemens Krauss's recommendation, correcting it from the vocal score where necessary. For the lay-out, we followed the Hoffmann and Schuh edition of Hofmannsthal's text as far as possible, and we have also chosen to follow this edition in matters of punctuation and spelling. This was because their critical edition has the merit of a meticulous scholarship towards Hofmannsthal's text which the scores lack. The attentive reader will note discrepancies between the German of Hofmannsthal's *Complete Works* and that in vocal scores or record librettos, such as 'Euer', 'Eurer' and 'Eure' or 'besondern' and 'besondren'. In these cases, that is where singability is concerned, we have followed the text in the full score. Where singability is not in question, we follow the *Complete Works*: we give 'k's for 'c's (in Chokolade, for instance) and Hofmannsthal's different style of capitalisation for two passages in Act Two which are not in the main body of his libretto in the *Complete Works* (the Octavian/Sophie duet 'Mit Ihren Augen' and the chorus of Lerchenau's servants

'Wenn ich Dich erwisch'). Hofmannsthal was inconsistent in his very sparing use of the apostrophe: sometimes, for example, the name Marie Theres appears with a final apostrophe, and more usually not. Peculiar divergences between the text of the full score and the *Complete Works* libretto have been footnoted.

The English is credited to Alfred Kalisch, the first and (to date) only English translator of the opera, but it has been extensively revised for performance by English National Opera in 1994. The passages which are very often cut, and which we do not perform, have not been revised and we have been content to make the English consistent in lay-out and to leave the reader to notice how free is his rendering of the German. The elaborate stage-directions are basically given in Kalisch's translation.

THE CHARACTERS

The Feldmarschallin *Princess of Werdenberg*	soprano
Octavian *called Quinquin, a young gentleman of noble family*	soprano
The Princess's Footmen	2 tenors, 2 basses
Baron Ochs of Lerchenau	bass
Major-Domo to the Princess	tenor
A Noble Widow	mezzo-soprano
Three Noble Orphans	2 sopranos 1 mezzo-soprano
A Milliner	soprano
An Animal Seller	tenor
A Notary	bass
Valzacchi *an intriguer*	tenor
Annina *his accomplice*	mezzo-soprano
A Tenor	tenor
Herr von Faninal *a rich merchant, newly ennobled*	baritone
Sophie *his daughter*	soprano
Marianne Leitmetzerin *Sophie's Duenna*	soprano
Major-Domo to Faninal	tenor
A Doctor	bass
A Landlord	tenor
A Commissar of Police	baritone

Pages to the Princess and Octavian, Hairdressers, a Flute Player, Leupold and Ochs's Retinue, Waiters, a Scholar, a Cook and Assistant, Notary's Assistant, Maidservants, Footmen, Suspicious Personages, Children, Musicians, Coachmen and Constables.

The action takes place in Vienna, during the first years of the reign of Maria Theresa.

Act One

Introduction [1, 2, 3, 4, 5, 6] The Marschallin's bedroom. To the left in the alcove the large tent-shaped four poster. Next to the bed, a three-leaved Chinese screen, behind which some clothes are lying. In addition, a little table and some chairs. On a little sofa to the left lies a sword in its sheath. To the right, great folding doors leading to the antechamber. In the centre, scarcely visible, a small door in the wall. No other doors. Between the alcove and the small door a dressing table and a few armchairs against the wall. The curtains of the bed are half-drawn. Through the half-open windows the bright morning sun streams in. From the garden birdsong can be heard.

Octavian kneels on a footstool, half embracing the Marschallin who is reclining in bed. Her face is hidden; only her beautiful hand and arm, peeping out from the sleeve of her lace nightgown, can be seen.

OCTAVIAN
(passionately)

How you were! How you are!	[7] Wie du warst! Wie du bist!
No one knows it, all your kindness!	Das weiss niemand, das ahnt keiner!

MARSCHALLIN
(raises herself on her pillow)

Do you reproach me for that, Quinquin?	Beklagt Er sich über das, Quinquin?
Would you have all the world share them?	Möcht' Er, dass viele das wüssten?

OCTAVIAN
(ardently)

Angel! No! Blessed am I,	Engel! Nein! Selig bin ich,
for it is I alone who knows your secrets!	dass ich der einzige bin, der weiss, wie du bist.
Knows your treasures! Knows your treasures!	Keiner ahnt es! Niemand weiss es.
You, you, you—Why talk of 'you'?	Du, du, du—was heisst das 'du'?
This 'You and I'?	Was 'du und ich'?
Do we know what they mean?	Hat denn das einen Sinn?
They are words, merely words—Yes—	Das sind Worte, blosse Worte, nicht?
You know.	Du sag'!
All the same though, there is something	Aber dennoch: Es ist etwas in ihnen,
within them, a feeling, a craving,	ein Schwindeln, ein Ziehen, ein Sehnen und Drängen,
a yearning, a striving,	
a longing, a burning:	ein Schmachten und Brennen:
my hand reaches out to search for your hand,	Wie jetzt meine Hand zu deiner Hand kommt,
and I must touch you, I want to hold you.	das Zudirwollen, das Dichumklammern,
All I want is only you;	das bin ich, das will zu dir,
but then that 'I' is lost in that 'You' . . .	aber das Ich vergeht in dem Du . . .
I am your heart—but then when I	Ich bin dein Bub—aber wenn mir dann
am carried away in your arms—	Hören und Sehen vergeht—
where is then your heart?	wo ist dann dein Bub?

MARSCHALLIN
(softly)

You are my heart, you are my love!	Du bist mein Bub, du bist mein Schatz!

(very tenderly)

I love you so!	Ich hab' dich lieb!

They embrace. [6]

OCTAVIAN
(starts up)

Why is it day? It shall not be day!	Warum ist Tag? Ich will nicht den Tag!
What use is the day?	Für was ist der Tag?
Then everyone sees you. Dark it shall be!	Da haben dich alle! Finster soll sein!

(He rushes to the window, closes it, and draws the curtains; the distant tinkling of a bell is heard. The Marschallin laughs to herself.) [8]

Why do you laugh?	Lachst du mich aus?

MARSCHALLIN
(tenderly)

Why do I laugh?	Lach ich dich aus?

49

OCTAVIAN

Angel!	Engel!

MARSCHALLIN

Dearest, my little boy!	Schatz du, mein junger Schatz!

(again a discreet tinkling)

Hark!	Horch!

OCTAVIAN

I will not.	Ich will nicht.

MARSCHALLIN

Hush, be still!	Still, pass auf.

OCTAVIAN

I will not listen! What can it be?	Ich will nichts hören! Was wirds denn sein?

(The sound comes closer.)

Is it footmen with letters, and pretty verses?	Sind's leicht Laufer mit Briefen und Komplimenten?
From Saurau, from Hartig, or the Portuguese Ambassador?	Vom Saurau, vom Hartig, vom portugieser Envoyé?
Here no one enters but I! I am master here!	[1] Hier kommt mir keiner herein! Hier bin ich der Herr!

The little door at the centre opens and a little Black Boy in yellow, hung with silver bells, trips across the room bearing a salver with chocolate. Invisible hands close the door behind him.

MARSCHALLIN

Ah, go and hide yourself, my breakfast comes.	Schnell, da versteck Er sich! Das Frühstück ist's.

(Octavian steps behind the screen.)

Put your sword over there behind the bed.	Schmeiss Er doch Seinen Degen hinters Bett.

(Octavian makes a dash for his sword and hides it. The Marschallin lies down again, after drawing the curtains. The Black Boy places the tray on the little table, pushes it to the front of the stage, pulls up the sofa and makes a deep obeisance to the Marschallin, with his arms crossed over his chest. Then he dances daintily backwards, with his face always turned to the Marschallin. At the door he bows again and vanishes. [9] The Marschallin appears from behind the bed curtains. She has wrapped a light fur-trimmed dressing-gown around her. Octavian reappears between the wall and the screen.)

You scatterbrain! What were you thinking of?	Er Katzenkopf, Er unvorsichtiger!
Gentlemen do not leave their swords lying in the room of a lady of fashion.	Lässt man in einer Dame Schlafzimmer seinen Degen herumliegen?
You should go to school again to learn your manners.	Hat Er keine besseren Gepflogenheiten?

OCTAVIAN

But if my manners are not to your taste,	[1] Wenn Ihr zu dumm ist, wie ich mich benehm',
if it offends you that I've no experience in matters such as this,	und wenn Ihr abgeht, dass ich kein Geübter in solchen Sachen bin,
why then, I have no notion how I am to please.	dann weiss ich überhaupt nicht, was Sie an mir hat!

MARSCHALLIN

(tenderly, from the sofa)

| Now don't philosophize, my Love, and come to me. | Philosophier Er nicht, Herr Schatz, und komm' Er her. |
| Now let's have breakfast. Everything in its own time. | Jetzt wird gefrühstückt. Jedes Ding hat seine Zeit. |

Octavian seats himself beside her. They are very tender over breakfast. Octavian buries his face in her lap. She strokes his hair. He looks up at her. [10]

OCTAVIAN

(softly)

Marie Theres'!	[4] Marie Theres'!

MARSCHALLIN

Octavian!	Octavian!

OCTAVIAN

Bichette!	Bichette!

	MARSCHALLIN
Quinquin!	Quinquin!
	OCTAVIAN
My heart!	Mein Schatz!
	MARSCHALLIN
My love!	Mein Bub!

They continue breakfast.

OCTAVIAN
(merrily)

The Feldmarschall is in Franconian woods	Der Feldmarschall sitzt im crowatischen
and hunts for bear and wild boar.	Wald und jagt auf Bären und Luchsen—
And I, I stay here in all my youth,	und ich, ich sitz hier, ich junges Blut,
and hunt for what?	und jag' auf was?
Ah, what a joy! Ah, what a joy!	Ich hab ein Glück, ich hab ein Glück!

MARSCHALLIN
(a shadow flitting across her face)

Oh leave the Feldmarschall in peace!	Lass Er den Feldmarschall in Ruh!
I dreamt of him last night.	Mir hat von ihm geträumt.

OCTAVIAN

Last night! You dreamt of him	Heut' Nacht hat dir von ihm geträumt?
last night? Last night?	Heut' Nacht?

MARSCHALLIN

My dreams, they are not mine to command.	Ich schaff mir meine Träume nicht an.

OCTAVIAN

Do you mean you really dreamt of him last	Heute Nacht hat dir von deinem Mann
night? Last night?	geträumt? Heute Nacht?

MARSCHALLIN

Don't stare so, don't be angry, it's no fault	Mach' Er nicht solche Augen. Ich kann
of mine.	nichts dafür.
I dreamt that he came home again.	Er war einmal wieder zuhaus.

OCTAVIAN
(softly)

The Feldmarschall?	Der Feldmarschall?

MARSCHALLIN

There was a noise below of horse and hound,	Es war ein Lärm im Hof von Pferd' und
and he was here.	Leut' und er war da.
With fright I started up in haste. Just	Vor Schreck war ich auf einmal wach, nein
see now,	schau nur,
see what a child I am: I still can hear it, all	schau nur, wie ich kindisch bin: ich hör'
the noise below.	noch immer den Rumor im Hof.
It's ringing in my ears. Don't you hear	Ich brings nicht aus dem Ohr. Hörst du
something?	leicht auch was?

OCTAVIAN

Yes, something I can hear, but why should	Ja freilich hör' ich was, aber muss es denn
it be your husband?	dein Mann sein!
Only think a moment, he's far away now,	Denk' dir doch, wo der ist: im Raitzenland
hunting in the mountains.	noch hinterwärts von Esseg.

MARSCHALLIN

Is it really so far?	Ist das sicher sehr weit?
Then what we hear is something else.	Na dann wird's halt was anders sein.
And all is well.	Dann is ja gut.

OCTAVIAN

You seem so anxious still, Theres'.	Du schaust so ängstlich drein, Theres'!

MARSCHALLIN

Listen, Quinquin, although he's far away,	Weiss Er, Quinquin—wenn es auch weit
	ist—
the Feldmarschall travels like the wind.	der Feldmarschall ist halt sehr geschwind.
But once . . .	Einmal—

She pauses.

OCTAVIAN

What happened once?	Was war einmal?

(The Marschallin listens, abstractedly. Octavian continues jealously.)

What happened once? Bichette,   Was war einmal, Bichette!
Bichette, what happened once?   Bichette! Was war einmal?

MARSCHALLIN

Ah, do be good, must you know all my   Ach sei Er gut, Er muss nicht alles wissen!
  secrets?

OCTAVIAN

You trifle with my heart!   So spielt sie sich mit mir!
(He throws himself in despair onto the sofa.)
I am a poor miserable wretch!   Ich bin ein unglücklicher Mensch!

MARSCHALLIN
(listening)

Do calm yourself. Be still. It is the   Jetzt trotz Er nicht. Jetzt gilt. Es ist der
  Feldmarschall.   Feldmarschall.
For, were a stranger there, the noise would   Wenn es ein Fremder wär', so wär' der
  surely be out there in the antechamber.   Lärm da draussen in meinem Vorzimmer!
It is my husband, now climbing up the   Es muss mein Mann sein, der durch die
  private staircase,   Garderob' herein will
and forcing the footmen to give way.   und mit den Lakaien disputiert!
Quinquin, my husband's here!   Quinquin, es ist mein Mann.
(Octavian draws his sword and runs to the right.)
Not there; that is the antechamber.   Nicht dort. Dort ist das Vorzimmer.
There sits a crowd of my dependents and   Da sitzen meine Lieferanten und ein halbes
  a score of lackeys are waiting.   Dutzend Lakaien.
There!   Da!
(Octavian runs to the small door.)
Too late! They're coming up the private   Zu spät! Sie sind schon in der Garderob'!
  stairs.
One chance remains,   Jetzt bleibt nur eins!
go hide yourself!   Versteck' Er sich!
(after a brief pause of indecision)
There!   Dort!

OCTAVIAN

I will not let him pass! I stay by you!   Ich spring' ihm in den Weg! Ich bleib' bei dir.

MARSCHALLIN

There by the bed! There in the curtains!   Dort hinters Bett! Dort in die Vorhäng'.
  And do not move!   Und rühr' dich nicht!

OCTAVIAN
(hesitating)

If I am caught, what will become of you,   Wenn er mich dort erwischt, was wird aus
  Theres'?   dir, Theres?

MARSCHALLIN
(pleading)

Hide quickly now, my love!   Versteck Er sich, mein Schatz.

OCTAVIAN
(by the screen)

Theres'!   Theres!
He vanishes between the screen and the alcove wall.

MARSCHALLIN
(stamping her feet impatiently)

Only stay still!   Sei Er ganz still!
(with flashing eyes)
Now we shall see   Das möcht' ich seh'n,
if he dares to force his way inside while I   ob einer sich dort hinüber traut, wenn ich
  am here.   hier steh'.
I'm no faint-hearted Italian Brigadier: Ich bin kein napolitan'scher General:
  Where I stand, I stand.   Wo ich steh', steh' ich.
(She goes with determination to the small door and listens.)
They're worthy fellows standing outside   Sind brave Kerl'n, meine Lakaien. Wollen
  there. They will not let him in to me,   ihn nicht herein lassen,
saying I'm asleep. Most worthy fellows!   sagen, dass ich schlaf. Sehr brave Kerl'n!
(The noise outside grows louder. She listens.)

That voice!	Die Stimm'!
That is not, surely, that's not my husband's voice!	Das ist ja gar nicht die Stimm' vom Feldmarschall!
They're saying 'Herr Baron' to him. It is a stranger.	Sie sagen 'Herr Baron' zu ihm! Das ist ein Fremder.

(gaily)

Quinquin, it is someone else.	Quinquin, es ist ein Besuch!

(She laughs.)

Quickly find your clothes, Octavian,	Fahr' Er schnell in seine Kleider,
but in hiding remain,	aber bleib' Er versteckt,
so that the footmen do not see you.	dass die Lakaien Ihn nicht seh'n.
That foolish, loutish voice, surely I should know it.	Die blöde, grosse Stimm' müsste ich doch kennen.
Who can it be? Mon Dieu, it surely is Ochs,	Wer ist denn das? Herrgott, das ist ja der Ochs.
it is my cousin of Lerchenau, it's Ochs of Lerchenau.	Das ist mein Vetter, der Lerchenau, der Ochs aus Lerchenau.
What does he want? Heavens above us!	Was will denn der? Jesus Maria!

(She laughs.)

Quinquin, listen. Quinquin, you cannot have forgot,	Quinquin, hört Er? Quinquin, erinnert Er sich nicht?
one day a letter was brought—	Vor fünf, sechs Tagen den Brief—
we were alone in my carriage—	Wir sind im Wagen gesessen,
and someone came galloping up with a letter in his hand.	und einen Brief haben sie mir an den Wagenschlag gebracht.
That letter came from Ochs;	Das war der Brief vom Ochs.
and now I have entirely forgotten what it said.	Und ich hab' keine Ahnung, was drin gestanden ist.

(She laughs.)

And you alone are the culprit, Quinquin.	Daran ist Er allein schuldig, Quinquin.

VOICE OF THE MAJOR-DOMO
(outside)

Herr Baron, will you be pleased to wait in the gallery.	Belieben Euer Gnaden in der Galerie zu warten!

During the next speeches the small doors at the back are pulled ajar several times and shut again, as if someone was trying to force his way in, and someone else was preventing him.

VOICE OF THE BARON
(outside)

Where did you learn such manners as these?	Wo hat Er Seine Manieren gelernt?
Herr Baron Lerchenau can't be kept waiting.	Der Baron Lerchenau antichambriert nicht.

MARSCHALLIN

Quinquin, where are you now? Where have you gone?	Quinquin, was treibt Er denn? Wo steckt Er denn?

OCTAVIAN

(coming out in a skirt and short jacket, his hair bound with a kerchief and ribbon, and making a curtsey) [11]

Your Ladyship's servant! I've not been long in your Highness's household here.	Befehl'n fürstli' Gnad'n, i' bin halt' noch nit recht lang in fürstli'n Dienst.

MARSCHALLIN

Quinquin!	Du, Schatz!
And only one kiss may I give you.	Und nicht einmal mehr als ein Busserl
That's for your wages.	kann ich dir geben.

(She kisses him quickly. There is more noise outside.)

He's hammering the door down, my dear cousin.	Er bricht mir ja die Tür ein, der Herr Vetter.
Quickly you must be off now,	Mach Er, dass Er hinauskomm'.
boldly march by all the footmen there.	Schlief' Er frech durch die Lakaien durch.
You're such a clever little rogue!	Er ist ein blitzgescheiter Lump! Und
But come back soon, my love,	komm' Er wieder, Schatz.
but be in men's clothing and through the proper door, come when you like.	Aber in Mannskleidern und durch die vordre Tür, wenn's Ihm beliebt.

53

She sits down on the sofa on her left with her back to the door and begins to drink her chocolate. Octavian hurries to the small door and tries to leave by it, but at the same moment the door is flung open, and Baron Ochs enters, the footmen trying in vain to keep him back. Octavian lowers his head and tries to escape quickly, but collides with him, and backs up to the wall on the left in confusion. Three footmen have entered with the Baron, and stand at a loss.

BARON
(pompously to the footmen)

I'm quite certain, of course she will receive me.

(He comes forward, while the footmen on his left try to bar his passage. [12])
(to Octavian with interest)

Pardon, my pretty child.

(Octavian in confusion turns his face to the wall.)
(graciously and with condescension)

I said, 'Pardon, my pretty child.'

(The Marschallin looks over her shoulder, rises, and goes to meet the Baron, who addresses Octavian gallantly.)

I really didn't mean to frighten you.

Selbstverständlich empfängt mich Ihro Gnaden.

Pardon, mein hübsches Kind!

Ich sag': Pardon, mein hübsches Kind.

Ich hab' Ihr doch nicht ernstlich weh getan?

THE THREE FOOTMEN
(attracting the Baron's attention, softly)

Her Most Excellent Highness!

Ihre fürstlichen Gnaden!

They take up their position in a tight row near the Marschallin, right in front of the small doors. The Baron makes an obeisance in the French manner, repeating it twice.

MARSCHALLIN

My dear cousin, you're looking well today.

Euer Liebden sehen vortrefflich aus.

BARON
(bows again, then to the footmen)

See what I told you, she is highly delighted that I came.

Sieht Er jetzt wohl, dass Ihre Gnaden entzückt ist, mich zu seh'n.

(The Baron goes towards the Marschallin with the bearing of a man of the world, giving her his hand and leading her forward.)

(quietly)

And why should Your Highness not be pleased!
Time is so unimportant when one's a person of rank.
Have I not morning after morning

visited our dear Princess Brioche, just to pay my respects to her,
while in her bath she sat at ease,
with nothing except a tiny silk screen between her and me?
I am astounded—

Und wie sollten Eure Gnaden nicht.

Was tut die frühe Stunde unter Personen von Stand?
Hab' ich nicht seinerzeit wahrhaftig Tag für Tag
uns'rer Fürstin Brioche meine Aufwartung gemacht,
da sie im Bad gesessen ist,
mit nichts als einem kleinen Wandschirm zwischen ihr und mir.
[13] Ich muss mich wundern,

(looking angrily around)

that any lackey dare—

wenn Euer Gnaden Livree—

Octavian would like to have slipped out in the meantime; the astonished glances of the footmen force him to be extremely cautious, and with affected ease he make his way along the wall to the alcove.

MARSCHALLIN

Forgive them, please,
my orders were given, they have obeyed them.
I suffered this morning from a migraine.

Verzeihen Sie,
man hat sich betragen, wie es befohlen.

Ich hatte diesen Morgen die Migräne.

At a sign from the Marschallin, the footmen have brought the two small sofas forward and retired. Octavian busies himself about the bed as inconspicuously as possible. The Marschallin seats herself on the sofa on the right after offering the Baron the sofa on the left.

BARON
(trying to sit down, much distracted by the presence of the pretty maid. Aside)

A pretty wench! A wholesome, luscious handful!

Ein hübsches Ding! Ein gutes, saub'res Kinderl!

The Marschallin rises and ceremoniously again offers him a seat. The Baron seats himself with hesitation, trying not to turn his back completely on the pretty maid. In the ensuing dialogue he turns sometimes towards the Marschallin, on his left, and sometimes to Octavian, on his right.

MARSCHALLIN

And even now I'm not quite well.   Ich bin auch jetzt noch nicht ganz wohl.
My dear Cousin, bearing that in mind, will   Der Vetter wird darum vielleicht die Gnade
   you have the kindness—   haben—

BARON

Why surely.   Natürlich.

He turns to his right to look at Octavian.

MARSCHALLIN

It's my waiting woman, a young girl from   Meine Kammerzofe, ein junges Ding vom
   the country.   Lande.
I'm afraid, though, her manners may not   Ich muss fürchten, sie inkommodiert Euer
   please Your Lordship.   Liebden.

BARON
(facing right)

She's very sweet!   Ganz allerliebst!

(facing left)

What? She does not please me! Me? The   Wie? Nicht im geringsten! Mich? Im
   contrary!   Gegenteil!

(He beckons Octavian with his hand. Then to the Marschallin)

But Your Highness perhaps was surprised   Euer Gnaden werden vielleicht verwundert
   to learn that I'm to be a bridegroom—   sein, dass ich als Bräutigam—

(looking to his left)

but yet, meanwhile—   indes—inzwischen—

MARSCHALLIN

A bridegroom?   Als Bräutigam?

BARON
(to his left)

Yes, I wrote it all in the letter that I sent to   Ja, wie Euer Gnaden denn doch aus
   Your Highness—   meinem Brief genugsam—

(to his right)

a rascal, very juicy, just a babe in arms.   ein Grasaff, appetitlich, keine fünfzehn
                                                 Jahr'!

MARSCHALLIN
(relieved)

You wrote a letter. Why, of course, and   Der Brief, natürlich, ja, der Brief, wer ist
   who's the lucky bride to be?   denn nur die Glückliche,
I have forgotten for the moment.   ich hab' den Namen auf der Zunge.

BARON
(to his left)

Eh?   Wie?

(over his shoulder)

Fresh as paint! So clean! So healthy! What   Pudeljung! Gesund! Gewaschen! Aller-
   a wench!   liebst!

MARSCHALLIN

But tell me who's the bride?   Wer ist nur schnell die Braut?

BARON

Sophie Faninal. But Your Highness,   [14] Das Fräulein Faninal. Habe Euer
I did not keep her name a secret.   Gnaden den Namen nicht verheimlicht.

MARSCHALLIN

Forgive me. My memory is at fault. What of   Natürlich! Wo hab' ich meinen Kopf?
   her family? They do not come from here?   Bloss die Famili. Sinds keine Hiesigen?

Octavian busies himself with the tray, and thus gets himself behind the Baron.

BARON

I assure Your Highness, yes, they come from   Jawohl, Euer Gnaden, es sind Hiesige.
   here.
One which Her Majesty the Queen has   Ein durch die Gnade Ihrer Majestät
   raised to noble rank.   Geadelter.
They have the contract now for the supplies   Er hat die Lieferung für die Armee, die in
   of all our armies in the West.   den Niederlanden steht.

(The Marschallin makes impatient signs to Octavian to withdraw.)
(The Baron completely misunderstands her expressions.)

I see that Your Highness shows upon her brow disdain at the misalliance.
And yet, I have to say it, the girl's as pretty as an angel from above.
She comes straight from a convent. She's an only child.

(more emphatically)

Her father possesses twelve houses in the city and has a palace too.
He's not over-healthy,

(chuckling)

or so I've heard it said.

Ich seh', Euer Gnaden runzeln Dero schöne Stirn ob der Mesalliance.
Allein, dass ich es sage, das Mädchen ist für einen Engel hübsch genug.
Kommt frischwegs aus dem Kloster. Ist das einzige Kind.

Dem Mann gehören zwölf Häuser auf der Wied'n, nebst dem Palais am Hof,
und seine Gesundheit—

—soll nicht die beste sein.

MARSCHALLIN

Ah, my dear cousin, I can see now which way the wind is blowing.

Mein lieber Vetter, ich kapier' schon, wie viel's geschlagen hat.

She signals to Octavian to withdraw.

BARON

And if Your Highness will allow me,
it seems to me I come of such a highly born and noble family that you can say
my blood is blue enough for two, corpo di Bacco!
As my wife, she will have an enviable social status,
befitting her position, and as regards our children, if the
Queen should refuse to give them the golden keys of nobility— Va bene!
They'll still possess all the twelve cast-iron keys
to the twelve houses in the city for their consolation.

Und mit Verlaub, fürstliche Gnaden,
ich dünke mir gut's adeliges Blut genug im Leib zu haben für ihre Zwei.
Man bleibt doch schliesslich, was man ist, corpo di Bacco!
Den Vortritt, wo er ihr gebührt, wird man der Frau Gemahlin
noch zu verschaffen wissen, und was die Kinder anlangt, wenn sie denen
den goldnen Schlüssel nicht konzedieren werden— Va bene!
Sie werden sich mit den zwölf eisernen Schlüsseln
zu den zwölf Häusern auf der Wied'n zu getrösten wissen.

MARSCHALLIN

Of course, I'm sure no child of yours would ever find it
hard to endure such consolation.

Gewiss! O sicherlich, dem Vetter seine Kinder,
die werden keine Don Quichotten!

Octavian walks backwards with the tray towards the door.

BARON

Where are you going with that chocolate? Come back here now!
Wait! Pst, what is it?

Warum hinaus die Chokolade! Geruhen nur!
Da! Pst, wieso denn!

Octavian hesitates, averting his face.

MARSCHALLIN

Off, now with you!

Fort, geh' Sie nur!

BARON

If you will allow me, Your Highness,
I haven't had a bite today.

Wenn ich Euer Gnaden gestehe,
dass ich so gut wie nüchtern bin.

MARSCHALLIN
(with resignation)

Mariandel, bring it back, and wait upon His Lordship.

Mariandel, komm Sie her. Servier Sie Seiner Liebden.

Octavian comes back and serves the Baron from his right, so that the latter is again between the Marschallin and Octavian.

BARON
(taking a cup and helping himself)

I'm nearly starving, my dear cousin.
Sitting in my carriage since five o'clock.

So gut wie nüchtern, Euer Gnaden. Sitz' im Reisewagen seit fünf Uhr früh.

(to Octavian)

God, what a piece of flesh!	Recht ein gestelltes Ding!
Do not run away.	Bleib' Sie hier, mein Herz.
I've something more to tell you.	Ich hab' Ihr was zu sagen.

(to the Marschallin, aloud)

All my servants are here, huntsmen and grooms and footmen—	Meine ganze Livree, Stallpagen, Jäger, alles—

(eating voraciously)

They are all gathered in the courtyard with my almoner.	alles unten im Hof zusamt meinem Almosenier.

MARSCHALLIN

(to Octavian)

You may go.	Geh Sie nur.

BARON

(to Octavian)

Give me another biscuit. Stay a while.	Hat Sie noch ein Biskoterl? Bleib' Sie doch!

(aside)

You are the sweetest angel, child, a proper pet.	Sie ist ein süsser Engel, Schatz, ein sauberer.

(to the Marschallin)

We're on our way to the 'White Horse Inn' where I shall be staying till tomorrow morning—	Sind auf dem Wege zum 'Weissen Rosse', wo wir logieren, heisst bis übermorgen—

(aside to Octavian)

I'll stick at no expense if we—	Ich gäb' was Schönes drum, mit Ihr—

(to the Marschallin, very loud)

—tomorrow morning—	—bis übermorgen—

(quickly to Octavian)

Just you and I all alone together: Ah!	unter vier Augen zu scharmutzieren! Wie?

(The Marschallin laughs at Octavian's impudent playacting.)

(to the Marschallin)

Then we're invited to stay with Faninal.	Dann ziehen wir ins Palais von Faninal.
Beforehand I have to choose a fitting ambassador—	Natürlich muss ich vorher den Bräutigamsaufführer—

(angrily to Octavian)

will you wait a minute?—	will Sie denn nicht warten?—
to my well-endowed and lovely bride I will send him,	an die wohlgeborne Jungfer Braut deputieren,
with the silver rose in his hand	der die Silberrose überbringt
as the old custom is among noblemen.	nach der hochadeligen Gepflogenheit.

MARSCHALLIN

And whom of all our kinsfolk has Your Lordship's choice fallen onto to act as his ambassador?	Und wen von der Verwandtschaft haben Euer Liebden für dieses Ehrenamt auserseh'n?

BARON

It is only because I need Your Highness' counsel on this question	Die Begierde, darüber Euer Gnaden Ratschlag einzuholen,
that I have made so bold to come so early and in my travelling attire—	hat mich so kühn gemacht, in Reisekleidern bei Dero heutigem Lever—

MARSCHALLIN

You wish?	Von mir?

BARON

To beg humbly the favour that I asked for in my letter.	Gemäss brieflich in aller Devotion getaner Bitte.
I hope I don't presume too much, that with my request I have given offence to you—	Ich bin doch nicht so unglücklich mit dieser devotesten Supplik Dero Missfallen—

(leaning back, to Octavian)

You could do with me anything you wanted. You're just the one for me!	Sie könnte aus mir machen, was Sie wollte. Sie hat das Zeug dazu!

MARSCHALLIN

How so, of course not.	Wie denn, natürlich!
We must find someone	Einen Aufführer
to be ambassador and call upon your bride,	für Euer Liebden ersten Bräutigamsbesuch,

one of our kinsfolk—whom to choose?	aus der Verwandtschaft—wen denn nur?
Our cousin Preysing? Well! Or cousin Lamberg?	Den Vetter Preysing? Wie? Den Vetter Lamberg*?
I wonder—	Ich werde—

BARON

I leave it to Your Highness's absolute discretion.	Dies liegt in Euer Gnaden allerschönsten Händen.

MARSCHALLIN

It's well. Will you not come to supper, then, dear cousin?	Ganz gut. Will Er mit mir zu Abend essen, Vetter?
Let's say tomorrow, will you? I'll be prepared with suggestions.	Sagen wir morgen, will Er? Dann proponier' ich Ihm einen.

BARON

For such grace and kindness I thank Your Highness.	Euer Gnaden sind die Herablassung selber.

MARSCHALLIN
(rising)

And now . . .	Indes . . .

BARON
(aside)

You must come back again. I'll stay here till you do.	Dass Sie mir wiederkommt! Ich geh' nicht eher fort!

MARSCHALLIN
(to herself)

Oho!	Oho!

(aloud)

Stay where you are! And is that all now you wish to ask of me?	Bleib Sie nur da! Kann ich dem Vetter für jetzt noch dienlich sein?

BARON

I hesitate to ask,	Ich schäme mich bereits.
but I'd be grateful if I could use Your Highness' attorney	An Euer Gnaden Notari eine Rekommandation
if I may.	wäre mir lieb.
I need advice on my marriage deed.	Es handelt sich um den Eh'vertrag.

MARSCHALLIN

My attorney is coming this morning. Go to see, Mariandel,	Mein Notari kommt öfter des Morgens. Schau' Sie doch, Mariandel,
if by chance he's in the anteroom and waiting.	ob er nicht in der Antichambre ist und wartet.

BARON

Why send the girl away?	Wozu das Kammerzofel?
She really ought to be here and at your service.	Euer Gnaden beraubt sich der Bedienung
I'll not allow it.	um meinetwillen!

He holds her back.

MARSCHALLIN

Let her be, cousin, so that she may go.	Lass Er doch, Vetter, sie mag ruhig geh'n.

BARON
(eagerly)

Oh, I can't agree. Stay here now beside Her Ladyship.	Das geb' ich nicht zu. Bleib' Sie hier zu Ihrer Gnaden Wink.
'Twill not be long before a footman comes.	Es kommt gleich wer von der Livree herein!
Can't let you go unprotected, bless my soul,	Ich liess ein solches Goldkind, meiner Seel',
why, God knows what those lackeys might do to you.	nicht unter das infame Lakaienvolk.

He caresses Octavian.

---

* Lamberg according to Hofmannsthal and in the full score, but Lambert in the vocal score.

MARSCHALLIN

But Your Lordship is much too concerned.　Euer Liebden sind allzu besorgt.

Enter the Major-Domo.

BARON

There, what did I just say?　　　　　Da, hab' ich's nicht gesagt?
He's come here no doubt with a message for　Er wird Euer Gnaden zu melden haben.
you.

MARSCHALLIN
(to the Major-Domo)

Struhan, tell me, is my attorney in the　Struhan, hab' ich meinen Notari in der
anteroom waiting?　　　　　　　　Vorkammer warten?

MAJOR-DOMO

Yes, the attorney's waiting there, Your　Fürstliche Gnaden haben den Notari,
Highness,
likewise the steward, and likewise the chef,　dann den Verwalter, dann den Kuchelchef,
then His Excellence Silva sends to you　dann von Exzellenz Silva hergeschickt,
a singer and with him a flute player.　　ein Sänger mit einem Flötisten.
(drily)
And also all the customary riffraff.　　Ansonsten das gewöhnliche Bagagi.

BARON
(pushes his chair behind the Major-Domo's back, and tenderly takes the hand of the supposed chamber-maid; to Octavian)
Say, have you ever　　　　　　　　Hat Sie schon einmal
been with a cavalier in tête-à-tête　　mit einem Kavalier im Tête-à-tête
together at supper?　　　　　　　zu Abend gegessen?
(Octavian simulates embarrassment.)
No? I bet your eyes would open. Will you?　Nein? Da wird Sie Augen machen. Will Sie?

OCTAVIAN
(softly, in confusion)
I don't really know if I ought.　　　I' weiss halt nit, ob i dös derf.

The Marschallin observes the pair as she listens attentively to the Major-Domo, and cannot refrain from laughing. The Major-Domo bows and retires, thus exposing the two to the Marschallin's view.

MARSCHALLIN
(laughing, to the Major-Domo)
Let them wait there.　　　　　　Warten lassen.
(Exit Major-Domo; the Baron tries to appear at his ease, and assumes a serious air.)
(laughing)
My cousin's not, I fancy, wasting his　Der Vetter ist, ich seh es, kein
chances.　　　　　　　　　　Kostverächter.

BARON
(relieved)
With you, Your Highness,　　　　Mit Euer Gnaden
(breathing more freely)
one feels quite at ease. You're so free and easy　ist man frei daran. Da gibt's keine Flausen
there's no need for pretences,　　　und keine Etiquette und
and no po-faced manners and etiquette.　keine spanische Tuerei!

He kisses the Marschallin's hand.

MARSCHALLIN
(amused)
But when you're to be a bridegroom?　Aber wo Er doch ein Bräut'gam ist?

BARON
(half rising, leaning towards her) [17]
Is that any reason to live like a monk?　Macht das einen lahmen Esel aus mir?
Better to be like a hungry dog off on a　Bin ich da nicht wie ein guter Hund auf
good day's hunting　　　　　　einer guten Fährte?
and very hot on every scent, to left and right.　Und doppelt scharf auf jedes Wild nach
　　　　　　　　　　　　　links, nach rechts!

I see now you're a hunter, you make a task to follow the chase.	Ich sehe, Euer Liebden betreiben es als Profession.

BARON

That is my pleasure.	Das will ich meinen.
It's a fact I know of nothing to suit me better.	Wüsste nicht, welche mir besser behagen könnte.
Your Highness, I must commiserate with you, you can only know — oh how can I say —	Ich muss Euer Gnaden sehr bedauern, dass Euer Gnaden nur — wie drück' ich mich aus —
only know the feelings of one defending her virtue.	die verteidigenden Erfahrungen besitzen!
Parole d'honneur! But that's not a patch on the joys of the hunter.	Parole d'honneur! Es geht nichts über die von der anderen Seite!

MARSCHALLIN
(laughing)

I doubt it not, variety is the spice of life.	Ich glaube Ihm, dass die sehr mannigfaltig sind.

BARON

In the whole of the year, in the whole of the day, there is never—	Soviel Zeiten das Jahr, soviel Stunden der Tag, da ist keine—

MARSCHALLIN

Never?	Keine?

BARON

A time—	Wo nicht—

MARSCHALLIN

A time?	Wo nicht?

BARON

A time Cupid doesn't provide us with a feast for all to enjoy.	Wo nicht dem Knaben Kupido ein Geschenkerl abzulisten wär'.
So we men are no roosters and no stags,	Dafür ist man kein Auerhahn und kein Hirsch,
rather we are Lords of Creation,	sondern ist man Herr der Schöpfung,
no need to come into season for mating, begging your pardon!	dass man nicht nach dem Kalender forciert ist, halten zu Gnaden!
For example, in May it is just right for lover's delights	Zum Exempel der Mai ist recht lieb für's verliebte Geschäft,
(you ask any child)	das weiss jedes Kind,
but of course I say	aber ich sage:
better in August, June or July.	Schöner ist Juni, Juli, August.
We have nights then.	Da hat's Nächte!
To us at home in summer comes an army of girls from Bohemia; in a swarm they cross the border:	Da ist bei uns da droben so ein Zuzug von jungen Mägden aus dem Böhmischen herüber:
and it's pleasant sometimes to induce just two or three to stay with me till the autumn falls.	Ihrer zweie, dreie halt' ich oft bis im November mir im Haus, dann erst schick' ich sie heim.
They come at harvest time, nor do they refuse to work, whatever the task.	Zur Ernte kommen sie und sind auch ansonsten anstellig und gut,

(chuckling)

When it's done, they go home.—	dann erst schick' ich sie heim.—
And how they agree,	Und wie sich das mischt,
the active, lissom folk of Bohemia, sad and sweet,—	das junge runde böhmische Völkel, schwer und süss,
with those of our land, of true German stock,	mit denen im Wald, mit denen im Stall,
so different, sharp and sour	dem deutschen Schlag scharf und herb
like a northern wine—	wie ein Retzer Wein—
yet they agree so well!	wie sich das mischen tut!
And everywhere lovers are waiting and seeking each other,	Und überall steht was und lauert und schielt durch den Gattern,
and whispering sweet nothings in tenderest accents,	und schleicht zueinander und liegt beieinander

and everywhere all day	und überall singt was
and night joyfully singing	und schupft sich in den Hüften
and milking	und melkt was
and reaping	und mäht was
with a will, and dabbling in the burns and in the village pond.	und plantscht und plätschert was im Bach und in der Pferdeschwemm.

MARSCHALLIN
(much diverted)

And are you everywhere keeping a watch?	Und Er ist überall dahinter her?

BARON

Would I could be, like Jupiter, happy in a thousand disguises!	Wollt', ich könnt' sein wie Jupiter selig in tausend Gestalten,
I could use the whole thousand.	wär' Verwendung für jede!

MARSCHALLIN

What, even the bull? So crude would you be?	Wie, auch für den Stier? So grob will Er sein?
You should ride as a cloud in heaven and go sailing o'er the mountains	Oder möcht' Er die Wolken spielen und dahergesäuselt kommen
like a scented summer breeze.	als ein Streiferl nasse Luft?

BARON
(very gaily)

That depends, yes, it depends.	Je nachdem! alls je nachdem!
For women, look you, must be wheedled and captured in a thousand different ways.	Das Frauenzimmer hat gar vielerlei Arten, wie es will genommen sein.
For one is all humble and shy.	Da ist die demütige Magd.
The next, a limb of the Devil, straight from Hell,	Und da die trotzige Teufelskreatur,
clouts you and beats your brains out with a broomstick.	haut dir die schwere Stalltür an den Schädel—
Then the third, who giggling and sobbing will lose her head—	Und da ist, die kichernd und schluchzend den Kopf verliert,
that one I like—	die hab' ich gern,
and then another—look in her eyes—there's a devil, cold and repelling,	und jener wieder, der sitzt im Auge ein kalter, rechnender Satan.
bide but your time—sure, 'twill come— you'll discover how that devil is yielding and relenting.	Aber es kommt eine Stunde, da flackert dieses lauernde Auge, und der Satan,
And when his last venomous glances he darts at me	indem er ersterbende Blicke dazwischen schiesst,

(with gusto)

that flavours the banquet past believing.	der würzt mir die Mahlzeit unvergleichlich.

MARSCHALLIN

It's you that's a devil, on my soul!	Er selber ist einer, meiner Seel'!

BARON

Yet another—pray give me leave— whom no one will look at:	Und wär' eine, haben die Gnad, die keiner anschaut
in tatters and rags she slinks along,	im schmutzigen Kittel schlumpt sie her,
crouches 'mid ashes by the hearth—	hockt in der Asche hinterm Herd,
she, if the right hour have but struck for your wooing,	die, wo du sie angehst zum richtigen Stündl—
she's not wanting!	die hat's in sich!
A wild amazement— stunned and bewildered, halting	Ein solches Staunen! gar nicht Begreifenkönnen!
twixt fear and shame; at last she yields, like one distraught with excess of joy,	und Angst! und Scham! und auf die letzt so eine rasende Seligkeit,
to think that he, the master and lord so far descends to look upon her lowliness!	dass sich der Herr, der gnädige Herr! herabgelassen gar zu ihrer Niedrigkeit.

MARSCHALLIN

You know more than your A-B-C.	Er weiss mehr als das A B C.

BARON

Then there are others who want to be caught by stealth,	Da gibt es welche, die wollen beschlichen sein,

soft as the wind a-blowing through the
fresh cut hay.

sanft wie der Wind das frisch gemähte Heu
beschleicht.

The best one, by Gad,

Und welche—da gilts,

(to Octavian, who has put the tray back on the breakfast table, and during the foregoing come up close on the Baron's left in amusement)

like a tiger you jump on her back,
kick the milk stool away,
then she lies there defenceless.

wie ein Luchs hinterm Rücken heran
und den Melkstuhl gepackt,
dass sie taumelt und hinschlägt!

(chuckling complacently)

You must have hay stacked for comfort
close at hand.

Muss halt ein Heu in der Nähe dabei
sein.

Octavian bursts out laughing.

MARSCHALLIN

No! What a man! What victories!
Just leave the girl alone.

Nein! Er agiert mir gar zu gut!
Lass Er mir doch das Kind!

BARON

(to Octavian, without embarrassment)

Meanest of attics can never disarm me,
splendour of boudoir can never alarm me.

Weiss mich ins engste Versteck zu bequemen,*
weiss im Alkoven galant mich zu
benehmen.

Fain would I clothe me in scores of disguises,
for as many enterprises.
None comes amiss whether simple or
cunning,
luring me on, or my company shunning,
splendour of boudoir can never alarm me,

Hätte Verwendung für tausend Gestalten,
tausend Jungfern festzuhalten.
Wäre mir keine zu junge, zu herbe,**
keine zu niedrige, keine zu derbe!
Tät' mich für keinem Versteck nicht
schämen,

all are for me, naught can disarm me.

seh' ich was Lieb's, ich muss mir's nehmen.

OCTAVIAN

(instantly playing his role again)

No, I won't go courtin' with you,
I do not think it right,
mercy, what would my mother say!
Sure I should die of fright.
I don't know what you say,
I don't know why I should.
One thing I know is, 'tis for no good,
mercy, what would my mother say!
I'd be too scared for funning,
you look so bold and cunning,
I'd be too scared for funning.
Such sport leads many a poor girl to her
ruin!

Na, zu dem Herrn, da ging' i net,
da hätt' i an Respekt,
na was mir da passieren könnt',
da wir' i gar zu g'schreckt.
I wass net, was er meint,
i wass net, was er will.
Aber was z'viel is, das ist zuviel.
Na was mir da passieren könnt'.
Das is ja net zum sagen,
zu so an Herrn da ging' i net,
mir tat's die Red' verschlagen.
Da tät' sich unsereins mutwillig schaden.

(to the Marschallin)

I'm frightened, Your Highness, look what
he's doin'.

Ich hab' solche Angst vor ihm, fürstliche
Gnaden.

MARSCHALLIN

Ha! What a man! What victories!
Ha! What a hero! Ha! What a hero!
Let that child be, I say.

Nein, Er agiert mir gar zu gut!
Er ist ein Rechter! Er ist der Wahre!
Lass Er mir doch das Kind!

---

* The full score has entirely different text for these lines:

Weiss mich in Heu und Stroh zu
bequemen ...

I make myself comfortable in hay and
straw ...

**Hirscher und Hahnen geben mir Laune,
seh' ich Fasanen sauber sich paaren,
juckt's mich, gefiedert dazwischen zu
fahren.

Stags and cocks put me in the mood,
if I see peasants coupling,
I feel the urge to join in.

Tät' auf'm Baum und im Korn mich
bequemen,

Then I make myself comfortable in the tree
and in the corn.

But of a hundred I see each day,
there are ninety like him, 'tis still the same story,
they find there's one glory, in all that's unseemly!
And we, Heaven knows,—we feel all the sorrow,
we bear the hard blows,
but perchance women sin more deeply than men.
What manners are those!

(with feigned severity)

Now let the child be!

Er ist ganz wie die andern dreiviertel sind.
Wie ich Ihn so sehe, so seh' ich hübsch viele.
Das sind halt die Spiele, die euch convenieren!
Und wir, Herr Gott! Wir leiden den Schaden,
wir leiden den Spott,
und wir haben's halt auch net anders verdient.
Und jetzt sakerlott,

jetzt lass Er das Kind!

BARON
(letting go of Octavian and assuming a dignified manner again)

Would Your Highness give me that charming wench
to come to my intended bride as her servant?

Geben mir Euer Gnaden den Grasaff da
zu meiner künft'gen Frau Gemahlin Bedienung.

MARSCHALLIN

What? Take my little one? Tell me what for?
I'm sure your bride will have no need of her.
Such a choice she would wish to make unaided.

Wie, meine Kleine da? Was sollte die?
Die Fräulein Braut wird schon versehen sein
und nicht anstehn auf Euer Liebden Auswahl.

BARON

I never saw such a promising wench.
She has a drop of good blood in her.

Das ist ein feines Ding! Kreuzsakerlott!
Da ist ein Tropf gutes Blut dabei!

OCTAVIAN
(aside)

A drop of good blood!

Ein Tropf gutes Blut!

MARSCHALLIN

But Your Lordship is really most observant!

Euer Liebden haben ein scharfes Auge!

BARON

Of course.

Geziemt sich.

(confidentially)

I think it important that we persons of noble birth and breeding should look for noble blood in all our servants.
I have one here who's a bastard of mine.

Find' in der Ordnung, dass Personen von Stand in solcher Weise von adeligem Blut bedienet werden,
führ' selbst ein Kind meiner Laune mit mir.

OCTAVIAN
(still listening with much amusement, aside)

He's brought his own bastard?

Ein Kind seiner Laune?

MARSCHALLIN

What? And a girl too? I certainly hope not!

Wie? Gar ein Mädel? Das will ich nicht hoffen!

BARON
(emphatically)

No, it's a son—with all the Lerchenau features in his face.

Nein, einen Sohn: trägt Lerchenauisches Gepräge im Gesicht.

OCTAVIAN

It's a son!

Einen Sohn!

MARSCHALLIN

It's a son!

Einen Sohn!

BARON

He is my body-servant.

Halt ihn als Leiblakai.

MARSCHALLIN
(laughing)

His body-servant!

Als Leiblakai!

OCTAVIAN

His body-servant!

Als Leiblakai!

BARON

So if Your Highness should presently order me to deliver the silver rose to your hands,	Wenn Euer Gnaden dann werden befehlen, dass ich die silberne Rose darf Dero Händen übergeben,
it's my son who will be the one who will bring it.	wird er es sein, der sie heraufbringt.

MARSCHALLIN

I understand. But a moment I beg.	Soll mich recht freu'n. Aber wart' Er einmal.

(making a sign to Octavian)

Mariandel!	Mariandel!

BARON

Come now Your Highness, give me Mariandel? I really need her!	Geben mir Euer Gnaden das Zofel! Ich lass nicht locker.

MARSCHALLIN

Ah! Go and bring the miniature gold medallion.	Ei! Geh Sie und bring Sie das Medaillon her.

OCTAVIAN

(softly)

Therese, Therese, beware.	Theres! Theres, gib acht!

MARSCHALLIN

(as before)

Bring it quick. I know very well what I do.	Bring's nur schnell! Ich weiss schon, was ich tu'.

BARON

(looking after Octavian)

Gad, she could be a young princess. [15]	Könnt' eine junge Fürstin sein.

(conversationally)

As a gift for my bride I've brought an accurate copy	Hab' vor, meiner Braut eine getreue Kopie
of my pedigree; that should please her.	meines Stammbaums zu spendieren
Also a lock of the first Lord Lerchenau, a devout supporter of the church	nebst einer Locke vom Ahnherrn Lerchenau, der ein grosser Klosterstifter war
and honourable Lord Lieutenant and Governor	und Obersterblandhofmeister in Kärnten
of the Carinthian March.	und in der windischen Mark.

Octavian brings the miniature from the bed alcove.

MARSCHALLIN

Would Your Lordship care to have this gallant gentleman	Wollen Euer Gnaden leicht den jungen Herren da
to take the silver rose to your lady?	als Bräutigamsaufführer haben?

BARON

(in light conversational tone)

Without a glance I trust Your Highness.	Bin ungeschauter einverstanden!

MARSCHALLIN

(with slight hesitation)

It's my young cousin, the Count Octavian.	Mein junger Vetter, der Graf Octavian.

BARON

(still very courteously)

Who could wish a more distinguished envoy?	Wüsste keinen vornehmeren zu wünschen!
I shall be obliged beyond all words to His Lordship.	Wär' in Devotion dem jungen Herrn sehr verbunden!

MARSCHALLIN

(quickly)

Look at him well!	Seh' Er ihn an!

She holds the miniature towards him.

BARON

(looking first at the miniature, then at the maid)

How like they are!	Die Ähnlichkeit!

MARSCHALLIN

Ah, yes.	Ja, ja.

	BARON
It's the very spitting image.	Wie aus dem Gesicht geschnitten!

	MARSCHALLIN
It has caused me myself some surprise.	Hat mir auch schon Gedanken gemacht.

(pointing to the miniature)

Rofrano, the younger brother of the Marquis.	Rofrano, des Herrn Marchese zweiter Bruder.

	BARON
Octavian? Rofrano! It's no small thing, coming of such a house	Octavian? Rofrano! Da ist man wer, wenn man aus solchem Haus!

(pointing to the maid)

and even though it's by the kitchen door.	und wär's auch bei der Domestikentür!

	MARSCHALLIN
That is why I prefer her over all the rest.	Darum halt' ich sie auch wie was Besonderes.

	BARON
Most fitting.	Geziemt sich.

	MARSCHALLIN
Always in waiting on me.	Immer um meine Person.

	BARON
Quite right.	Sehr wohl.

	MARSCHALLIN
But get you gone now, Mariandel, off you go.	Jetzt aber geh' Sie, Mariandel, mach' Sie fort.

	BARON
What's that? She's coming back though?	Wie denn? Sie kommt doch wieder?

MARSCHALLIN
(intentionally ignoring the Baron)

Admit all who wait to see me outside.	Und lass Sie die Antichambre herein.

Octavian goes towards the folding door on the right.

BARON
(following him)

Most lovely child!	Mein schönstes Kind!

OCTAVIAN
(by the door on the right)

You can come in now!	Derfts eina gehn!

She runs to the other door.

BARON
(following him)

I am your humble servant. Let me have a word with you alone.	Ich bin Ihr Serviteur! Geb' Sie doch einen Augenblick Audienz!

OCTAVIAN
(slamming the door in the Baron's face)

In good time.	I komm glei.

At this moment an old Lady's Maid enters through the same door. The Baron retreats disappointed. Two footmen come from the left and bring a screen from the alcove. The Marschallin retires behind the screen, the Lady's Maid following her. The dressing-table is brought to the centre of the stage. Footmen open the folding door on the left. Enter the Notary, the Head-cook, followed by a scullion carrying the Menu Book. Then the Milliner, a Scholar with a huge tome, and the Animal Seller with tiny dogs and an ape. Valzacchi and Annina, slipping in quickly behind these, take the foremost place on the left. The Noble Widow with her three daughters take places on the right; all are in deep mourning. The Major-Domo leads the Singer and the Flute Player to the front. The Baron, in the background, makes a sign to a footman, gives him an order, and points, 'Here, through the back door'.

THREE NOBLE ORPHANS
(shrilly)

Three poor but noble little orphans —	Drei arme adelige Waisen —

(The Noble Widow signals to them not to shriek so, and to kneel down.)

Three poor but noble little orphans lie weeping at your Highness' feet.	Drei arme adelige Waisen erflehen Dero hohen Schutz!

MILLINER
(loudly)

Le chapeau Paméla! La poudre à la reine   Le chapeau Paméla! La poudre à la reine
de Golconde!   de Golconde!

ANIMAL SELLER

Pretty monkeys to tease your flunkeys,   Schöne Affen, wenn Durchlaucht schaffen,
bright parakeets and birds from Africa.   auch Vögel hab' ich da, aus Afrika.

THREE ORPHANS

Our father in youth died a glorious death   Der Vater ist jung auf dem Felde der Ehre
    for his country,   gefallen,
it is our fondest wish to do the same as he.   ihm dieses nachzutun, ist unser Herzensziel.

MILLINER
(loudly)

Le chapeau Paméla! C'est la merveille   Le chapeau Paméla! C'est la merveille
du monde!   du monde!

ANIMAL SELLER

Cockatoo and painted jay,   Papageien hätt' ich da
from India and Africa.   aus Indien und Afrika.
Puppies quite small,   Hunderln so klein
trained to prowess,   und schon zimmerrein.
never any mess.

The Marschallin steps out. All bow low. The Baron has come forward on the left.

MARSCHALLIN
(to the Baron)

I now present to you, dear cousin, my man   Ich präsentiere Euer Liebden hier den
    of law.   Notar.

The Notary, bowing towards the dressing-table at which the Marschallin has seated herself, steps towards the Baron on the left. The Marschallin summons the youngest of the three orphans to her side, takes a purse from the Major-Domo, gives it to the girl, and kisses her on the forehead. The Scholar tries to come forward and offer the Marschallin his book. Valzacchi darts in front of him and pushes him aside.

VALZACCHI
(flourishing a black-edged news-sheet) [18]

The scandal newspaper, Your Highness!   Die swarze Seitung! Fürstlike Gnade!
All the secret news and scandal!   alles 'ier geeim gesrieben!
Only given to famous people,   nur für 'ohe Persönlikeite!
the secret gossip.   die swarze Seitung!
There's a dead man in the anteroom of   eine Leikname in 'Interkammer
one of the ministers of state!   von eine gräflike Palais!
And a doctor's wife helping her lover   eine Bürgersfrau mit der amante
to poison her husband   vergiften den Hehemann!
last night at three o'clock.   diese Nackt um dreie Huhr!

MARSCHALLIN

Take your tales to the kitchen door!   Lass Er mich mit dem Tratsch in Ruh!

VALZACCHI

But Lady,   In Gnaden!
Tutte Quante are as true as de Bible   tutte quante Vertraulikeite
from de court and town.   aus die grosse Welt!

MARSCHALLIN

I will not listen! Take your tales   Ich will nix wissen! Lass Er mich mit
    to the kitchen door.   dem Tratsch in Ruh!

Valzacchi retreats with a regretful bow.

THREE ORPHANS
(They have each and, finally, their Mother kissed the Marschallin's hand, and are ready to leave.)
(in a whining tone)

Joy and blessing, all confessing,   Glück und Segen allerwegen Euer Gnaden
    lift their voices in your praise.   hohem Sinn!
We shall count the high-born bounty   Eingegraben steht erhaben er in unserm
    of Your Highness all our days!   Herzen drin!

Exeunt with their Mother.

The Hairdresser enters hastily, his Assistant rushing after him with coat-tails flying. The Hairdresser carefully scans the Marschallin; looks solemn; retreats. He is examining her looks today. In the meantime the Assistant at the dressing-table is unpacking. The Hairdresser pushes several people back so as to have more room. After a little consideration he forms his plan, bustles up to the Marschallin with decision, and begins to do her hair. Enter a footman in pink, black and silver bearing a note. The Major-Domo is at his hand with a silver salver, on which he presents it to the Marschallin. The Hairdresser stands back to allow her to read it. His Assistant hands him new tongs. The Hairdresser waves them to and fro to cool them. After a questioning glance at the Marschallin, who nods, the Assistant hands him the note. He smiles, and uses it to cool the tongs.

Meanwhile the Singer has taken up his position holding his music. The Flute Player accompanies him, watching him over his shoulder. Three Footmen are at the front on the right, the others stand in the background.

SINGER*

Di rigori armato il seno	[19]	Di rigori armato il seno
Contro amor mi ribellai		Contro amor mi ribellai
Ma fui vinto in un baleno		Ma fui vinto in un baleno
In mirar due vaghi rai.		In mirar due vaghi rai.
Ahi! che resiste puoco		Ahi! che resiste puoco
Cor di gelo a stral di fuoco.		Cor di gelo a stral di fuoco.

The Hairdresser hands the curling tongs to his Assistant and applauds the singer. Then he proceeds with arranging the Marschallin's curls. In the meantime a footman has admitted the Baron's Body-servant, Almoner and Huntsman by the small door.

It is a strange trio. The Body-servant is a tall young fellow with a foolish, insolent expression. He carries a jewel-case of red morocco under his arm. The Almoner is an unkempt village priest, four feet high, but a strong and impudent-looking imp. The Huntsman looks as if he had been carting dung before he was pushed into his ill-fitting livery. The Almoner and the Body-servant seem to be fighting for precedence, and trip each other up. They steer a course to the left, towards their Master, in whose vicinity they come to a halt.

BARON

(seated on the armchair at the front on the left, to the Notary who is standing in front of him taking instructions. In an undertone)

As compensation, quite as a separate gift,	Als Morgengabe—ganz separatim jedoch
before the dowry, you understand me, do you not?—	und vor der Mitgift—bin ich verstanden, Herr Notar?—
The house and lands of Gaunersdorf return to me!	kehrt Schloss und Herrschaft Gaunersdorf an mich zurück!
Redeemed of debt and with manorial rights undiminished	Von Lasten frei und ungemindert an Privilegien,
just as my father held them for his whole life long.	so wie mein Vater selig sie besessen hat.

NOTARY
(short of breath)

Your Lordship, it is my painful duty delicately to remind you	Gestatten Hochfreiherrliche Gnaden die submisseste Belehrung,
that such a compensation from the wife to the husband,	dass eine Morgengabe wohl vom Gatten an die Gattin,
instead of from the husband to the wife	nicht aber von der Gattin an den Gatten

(taking a deep breath)

by contract is not in law or custom possible.	bestellet und stipuliert zu werden fähig ist.

BARON

That may be so.	Das mag wohl sein.

NOTARY

It is so —	Das ist so —

BARON

But this is a special case —	Aber im besondren Fall —

---

* An English translation of this verse is:
  With my breast armed with hardness / I rebelled against love / but I was defeated in a flash / by two fleeting glances. / Ah! How could a / heart of ice resist a shaft of fire?

The law, sir, and its wise prescriptions, postulate no special case.	Die Formen und die Präskriptionen kennen keinen Unterschied.

BARON
(shouting)

Then it is time it began to!	Haben ihn aber zu kennen!

NOTARY

Your pardon!	In Gnaden!

BARON
(quietly again, but with insistence, and full of amour-propre)

If one who springs from the very [20] noblest stock should so far condescend as to take in marriage one almost of the middle classes like Miss Faninal — you understand me?—take her to his bed in fact before God and the world, and as one might say, under the eye of the Imperial court,	Wo eines hochadeligen Blutes blühender Spross sich herablässt, im Ehebette einer so gut als bürgerlich Mamsell Faninal —bin ich verstanden?—acte de présence zu machen vor Gott und der Welt und sozusagen angesichts kaiserlicher Majestät—

(The Flute Player begins his prelude again.)

Surely, corpo di Bacco! A compensation would only be common justice as a sign of thanks for the sacrifice I am making by giving my name to her.	da wird, corpo di Bacco! von Morgengabe als geziemendem Geschenk dankbarer Devotion für die Hingab' so hohen Blutes sehr wohl die Rede sein.

The Singer seems about to begin, but waits for the Baron to be silent.

NOTARY
(to the Baron in a low voice)

Perhaps, by way of a separate conveyance—	Vielleicht, dass man die Sache separatim—

BARON
(in a low voice)

You are a pettifogging fool! As compensation, I want my deeds back!	Er ist ein schmählicher Pedant: als Morgengabe will ich das Gütel!

NOTARY
(as before)

As an especial item in the marriage contract.	Als einen wohl verklausulierten Teil der Mitgift—

BARON
(a little louder)

As compensation! Will nothing get it through your thick skull?	Als Morgengabe! geht das nicht in seinen Schädel?

NOTARY
(in the same tone)

As a donation inter vivos or else . . .	Als eine Schenkung inter vivos oder—

BARON
(banging his fist on the table in a rage, and shouting)

As compensation!	Als Morgengabe!

SINGER*
(during the foregoing discussion)

Ma si caro è 'l mio tormento [19] Dolce è si la piaga mia Ch' il penare è mio contento E 'l sanarmi è tirannia Ahi! Che resiste puoco— Cor . . .	Ma si caro è 'l mio tormento Dolce è si la piaga mia Ch' il penare è mio contento E 'l sanarmi è tirannia Ahi! Che resiste puoco— Cor . . .

---

* But so dear to me is my torment, / so sweet is my anguish / that the suffering is my delight / and healing is tyranny.

At this point the Baron raises his voice to such a pitch that the Singer breaks off abruptly, as does the Flute Player. The Notary retires to a corner in alarm. The Marschallin summons the Singer and gives him her hand to kiss. The Singer and the Flute Player retire, bowing deeply. The Baron makes as if nothing had happened, waves condescendingly to the Singer, crosses over to his servants, straightens his Body-Servant's tousled hair; then goes to the small door as if looking for somebody, opens it, peeps out, is annoyed that the chamber-maid is not coming back; snoops about the bed, shakes his head, and comes forward again.

MARSCHALLIN
(looking at herself in her hand mirror, in an undertone)

My dear friend Hippolyte,	Mein lieber Hippolyte,
ah, look at me and see how old	heut' haben Sie ein altes Weib aus mir
you've made me look!	gemacht!

The Hairdresser falls, in consternation, on the Marschallin's coiffure with feverish energy, and changes it again. The Marschallin continues to look thoughtful. Valzacchi, followed by Annina, has slunk behind everyone else's backs to the other side of the stage, and now presents himself to the Baron with exaggerated obsequiousness.

MARSCHALLIN
(to the Major-Domo, over her shoulder)

Tell them all to go!	Abtreten die Leut!

The Footmen, taking hands, push them all out by the door, which they then close. Only the Scholar, whom the Major-Domo presents to the Marschallin, remains in conversation with her until the close of the episode between Valzacchi, Annina and the Baron.

VALZACCHI
(to the Baron)

De Barone needs my help I see,	[21] Ihre Gnade sukt etwas. Ik seh'.
de Barone is needing my service.	Ihre Gnade at eine Bedürfnis.
I can make me useful in all ways.	Ik kann dienen. Ik kann besorgen.

BARON
(retreating)

And what, sir, are you, sir?	Wer ist Er, was weiss Er?

VALZACCHI, ANNINA

De Barone 'e speak out of his eyes	Ihre Gnade Gesikt sprikt ohne Sunge.
like Italian marble. Come statua di Giove.	Wie eine Hantike: come statua di Giove.

ANNINA

Italian marble . . . di Giove . . .	Wie eine Hantike . . . di Giove . . .

BARON

A most remarkable man.	Das ist ein besserer Mensch.

VALZACCHI, ANNINA

My Lord Barone, we are both your obedient	Erlaukte Gnade, attachieren uns an sein
servant.	Gefolge!

He falls on his knees, as does Annina.

BARON

You?	Euch?

VALZACCHI, ANNINA

Uncle and niece.	Onkel und Nickte.
Together we do better work.	Su sweien maken alles besser.
Per esempio: De Barone's lady is very	Per esempio: Ihre Gnade at eine junge
young?	Frau—

BARON

And just how do you know, you rascal, you?	Woher weiss Er denn das, Er Teufel Er?

VALZACCHI, ANNINA
(eagerly)

De Barone is a jealous man: dico per dire!	Ihre Gnade ist in Eifersukt: dico per dire!
Now or tomorrow it may be. Affare nostro!	Eut oder morgen könnte sein. Affare nostro!
Every step de lady may make,	Jede Sritt die Dame sie tut,
every carriage de lady take,	jede Wagen die Dame steigt,
every letter de lady may get—	jede Brief die Dame bekommt—
we are there.	wir sind da!
Up de chimney or by de fire,	an die Ecke, in die Kamin,
under de carpet—or in de curtain,	in die Kommode, 'inter die Bette—

69

up in de attic or in a cupboard,	in eine Schranke, unter die Dache,
in de corner, under de bed—	
we are there!	wir sind da!

The Marschallin rises. The Hairdresser bows low, and hurries off followed by his Assistant.

ANNINA

| De Barone will not regret it! | Ihre Gnade wird nicht bedauern! |

They hold out their hands for money. He pretends not to notice.

BARON
(in an undertone)

Hm! What a life it is in this old town.	Hm! Was es alles gibt in diesem Wien!
I'll test you now: do you know that girl	Zur Probe nur. Kennt Sie die Jungfer
Mariandel?	Mariandel?

ANNINA
(in an undertone)

| Mariandel? | Mariandel? |

BARON
(in an undertone)

| The serving maid who waits there on Her | Das Zofel hier im Haus bei ihrer Gnaden. |
| Highness. | |

VALZACCHI
(in a whisper to Annina)

| Sai tu? Cosa vuole? | Sai tu? Cosa vuole? |

ANNINA
(also whispering)

| Niente! | Niente! |

VALZACCHI
(to the Baron)

Surely, surely, my niece knows	Sicker! Sicker! Meine Nickte wird
all about her,	besorgen!
be assured of that, Your Lordship.	Seien sicker, Ihre Gnade! Wir sind da!
We are there!	

He holds out his hand again. The Baron ignores him.

BARON
(leaving the two Italians; to the Marschallin)

| May I now introduce | [12] Darf ich das Gegenstück |

(discreetly)

| the counterpart of your Mariandel | zu Dero sauber'm Kammerzofel |
| to Your Highness? | präsentieren? |

(complacently)

| The likeness is, so I'm told, unmistakable. | Die Ähnlichkeit soll, hör' ich, |
| | unverkennbar sein. |

(The Marschallin nods.)

| Leopold, give me the case! | Leopold, das Futteral. |

The young footman presents the case awkwardly.

MARSCHALLIN
(smiling slightly)

| He does great honour to his ancestry. | Ich gratuliere Euer Liebden sehr. |

BARON
(taking the case from the lad, and signalling him to retire)

| And here I have the silver rose. | Und da ist nun die silberne Rose! |

He is about to open it. [14]

MARSCHALLIN

| Do not disturb it. | Lassen nur drinnen. |
| Put it down here, please, if you don't mind. | Haben die Gnad' und stellen's dorthin. |

BARON

| Or shall we call for your Mariandel? | Vielleicht das Zofel soll's übernehmen? |
| Let me ring. | Ruft man ihr? |

MARSCHALLIN

No, let her be. She has her duties too.	Nein, lassen nur. Die hat jetzt keine Zeit.
But this I promise: the Count Octavian	[6] Doch sei Er sicher: den Grafen Octavian
shall be informed.	bitt' ich Ihm auf,

70

For me he'll consent, I know, and will duly ride as cavalier to your bride and present her with the silver rose.	er wird's mir zulieb schon tun und als Euer Liebden Kavalier vorfahren mit der Rosen zu der Jungfer Braut.

(with indifference)

Leave it there if you will. And now, dear cousin, I must say Adieu. The time has come for all to leave, or I shall be too late for church.	Stellen indes nur hin. Und jetzt, Herr Vetter, sag' ich Ihm Adieu. Man retiriert sich jetzt von hier: Ich werd' jetzt in die Kirchen gehn.

The footmen open the folding doors.

BARON

Gracious Highness, you're too kind. Your overwhelming charms have touched my heart.	Euer Gnaden haben heut' durch unversiegte Huld mich tiefst beschämt.

He makes an obeisance and withdraws ceremoniously. At a signal from him the Notary follows him. His three servants shuffle awkwardly out. The two Italians silently and obsequiously join his train without his noticing them. The footmen close the door. The Major-Domo withdraws. The Marschallin is left alone.

MARSCHALLIN
(alone)

Ah there he goes, a vain, pretentious pompous fellow, and takes a young and lovely bride and ample dowry as reward.	Da geht er hin, der aufgeblas'ne, schlechte Kerl, und kriegt das hübsche, junge Ding und einen Pinkel Geld dazu,

(sighing)

He takes it all, and then he's pleased to think that he's the one who is honouring her! But why trouble myself? The world will have it so. I remember a girl, just like this one [22] who fresh from the convent was marched off straight to the holy estate of wedlock.	als müsst's so sein. Und bildet sich noch ein, dass er es ist, der sich was vergibt. Was erzürn' ich mich denn? 's ist doch der Lauf der Welt. Kann mich auch an ein Mädel erinnern, die frisch aus dem Kloster ist in den heiligen Eh'stand kommandiert word'n.

(She takes a hand mirror.)

Where is she now? Ah,	Wo ist die jetzt? Ja,

(sighing)

go, seek the sorrows of yesteryear! But can it be,	such dir den Schnee vom vergangenen Jahr. Das sag' ich so:

(quietly)

(ah yes, can it really be so) that I was that young girl long ago and that I shall one day become the old Princess . . . The old Princess, the Marshall's old Princess! 'Look now, there goes the old Princess Theresa!' How can this come to pass? Is this indeed the will of God? For I am still I, the very same. But if indeed it must be so, why then do I sit here looking on, and see it all, so clear? Why are these things not kept from me? This all is mystery, all mystery, and we are here on earth	Aber wie kann das wirklich sein, dass ich die kleine Resi war und dass ich auch einmal die alte Frau sein werd! Die alte Frau, die alte Marschallin! 'Siegst es, da geht die alte Fürstin Resi!' Wie kann denn das gescheh'n? Wie macht denn das der liebe Gott? Wo ich doch immer die gleiche bin. Und wenn er's schon so machen muss, warum lasst er mich zuschau'n dabei, mit gar so klarem Sinn? Warum versteckt er's nicht vor mir? Das alles ist geheim, so viel geheim. Und man ist dazu da,

(sighing)

to bear it all. [5] But to know 'how?'—	dass man's ertragt. Und in dem 'Wie'

(very quietly)

in that lies all the difference —	da liegt der ganze Unterschied —

(to Octavian who enters from the right in riding-dress and riding-boots; calmly, half smiling)

Ah! You are back again?	Ah! Du bist wieder da?

<table>
<tr><td></td><td>**OCTAVIAN**
(tenderly)</td></tr>
<tr><td>And you're unhappy.</td><td>Und du bist traurig!</td></tr>
</table>

MARSCHALLIN

The mood has flown away. You know me, how I am.	Es ist ja schon vorbei. Du weisst ja, wie ich bin.
One moment laughing, one moment crying.	Ein halb Mal lustig, ein halb Mal traurig.
My thoughts, I cannot command them, I know not why.	Ich kann halt meine Gedanken nicht kommandiern.

OCTAVIAN

I know why you have been in tears, my heart.	Ich weiss, warum du traurig bist, mein Schatz.
You were beside yourself and panic-stricken.	Weil du erschrocken bist und Angst gehabt hast.
Am I not right? Confess to me:	Hab' ich nicht recht? Gesteh' mir nur:
you were terrified,	Du hast Angst gehabt,
my angel, my loved one,	du Süsse, du Liebe.
my love, my love!	Um mich, um mich!

MARSCHALLIN

A little perhaps,	Ein biss'l vielleicht,
but I recovered my courage and to myself I said: now what indeed should I fear.	aber ich hab' mich erfangen und hab' mir vorgesagt: Es wird schon nicht dafür steh'n.
And does it really matter?	Und wär's dafür gestanden?

OCTAVIAN
(gaily)

It was not the Feldmarschall,	Und es war kein Feldmarschall.
but a silly clown, your cousin, and you are all mine,	Nur ein spassiger Herr Vetter und du gehörst mir.
you are all mine.	Du gehörst mir!

MARSCHALLIN
(pushing him aside)

Dearest, embrace me not so much.	Taverl, umarm' Er nicht zu viel:
Who tries to hold too much, holds nothing fast.	Wer allzuviel umarmt, der hält nichts fest.

OCTAVIAN
(passionately)

Say you are mine alone, mine!	Sag', dass du mir gehörst! Mir!

MARSCHALLIN

Oh! Do but be good, be tender and gentle and kind and wise.	Oh, sei Er jetzt sanft, sei Er gescheit und sanft und gut.

(Octavian is about to answer excitedly.)

I beg you, oh do not be like all the other men.	Nein, bitt' schön, sei Er nicht wie alle Männer sind.

OCTAVIAN
(starting up suspiciously)

Like all the others?	Wie alle Männer?

MARSCHALLIN
(quickly recovering herself)

Like the Feldmarschall and my cousin Ochs.	Wie der Feldmarschall und der Vetter Ochs.

OCTAVIAN
(still not satisfied)

Bichette!	Bichette!

MARSCHALLIN
(emphatically)

No, do not be like all the other men.	Sei Er nur nicht, wie alle Männer sind.

OCTAVIAN
(angrily)

I know nothing of the other men.	Ich weiss nicht, wie alle Männer sind.

(with sudden tenderness)

Only I know I love you.	Weiss nur, dass ich dich lieb hab',

Bichette, they've taken you away from me.	Bichette, sie haben dich mir ausgetauscht.
Bichette, where have you gone?	Bichette, wo ist Sie denn?

MARSCHALLIN
(calmly)

I am still here, my love.	Sie ist wohl da, Herr Schatz.

OCTAVIAN

Oh, when you're here, then I want to hold you,	Ja, ist Sie da? Dann will ich Sie halten,
to protect you from what may befall,	dass Sie mir nicht wieder entkommt!

(passionately)

hold you by my side, hold you.	Packen will ich Sie, packen, dass
Then you will know to whom you belong.	Sie es spürt, zu wem Sie gehört—
To me! For I am yours and you are mine!	zu mir! Denn ich bin Ihr und Sie ist mein!

MARSCHALLIN
(escaping from him)

Oh do be good, Quinquin. I feel I know	Oh sei Er gut, Quinquin. Mir ist zu Mut,
that all things earthly are but a vanity, vain empty dreams;	dass ich die Schwäche von allem Zeitlichen recht spüren muss,
deep in my heart I know	bis in mein Herz hinein:
how should we grasp at naught,	wie man nichts halten soll,
how can we cling to naught,	wie man nichts packen kann,
how life and its joys slip through our fingers,	wie alles zerläuft zwischen den Fingern,
how everything alters if we but grasp it,	wie alles sich auflöst, wonach wir greifen,
everything fades like shadows, like dreams.	alles zergeht, wie Dunst und Traum.

OCTAVIAN

My God, what do you say? You only want to tell me	Mein Gott, wie Sie das sagt, Sie will mir doch nur zeigen,
that you love me no more.	dass Sie nicht an mir hängt.

He weeps.

MARSCHALLIN

Ah, do be good, Quinquin!	Sei Er doch gut, Quinquin!

Octavian weeps even more bitterly.

Ah, now I am the one who must console him	Jetzt muss ich noch den Buben dafür trösten,
for the day, be it soon, be it late, when he will leave me.	dass er mich über kurz oder lang wird sitzen lassen.

She caresses him.

OCTAVIAN

'Be it soon, be it late',	Über kurz oder lang?

(angrily)

who could have put such words into your mouth, Bichette?	Wer legt dir heut' die Wörter in den Mund, Bichette?

MARSCHALLIN

Do my words hurt you so?	Dass Ihn das Wort so kränkt.

(Octavian stops his ears.)

The time is coming, Quinquin,	Die Zeit im Grunde, Quinquin, die Zeit,
the time, be it sooner or later, what matter.	die ändert doch nichts an den Sachen.
For time, how strangely goes its own way. [23]	Die Zeit, die ist ein sonderbar Ding.
We do not heed it, time has no meaning,	Wenn man so hinlebt, ist sie rein gar nichts.
but there comes a moment	Aber dann auf einmal,
when time is all we feel.	da spürt man nichts als sie:
All the world talks of it, all our souls are filled with it.	sie ist um uns herum, sie ist auch in uns drinnen.
On every face its mark will show. Each mirror betrays it,	In den Gesichtern rieselt sie, im Spiegel da rieselt sie,
all through my dreams it's flowing,	in meinen Schläfen fliesst sie.
and now between us two it flows in silence,	Und zwischen mir und dir da fliesst sie wieder.
trickling as in an hourglass.	Lautlos, wie eine Sanduhr.

(earnestly)

Oh Quinquin,	Oh Quinquin!
sometimes I hear it flowing	Manchmal hör' ich sie fliessen
unrelenting.	unaufhaltsam.

(softly)

Sometimes I arise in the dead of night,	Manchmal steh' ich auf, mitten in der Nacht
go to my clocks and stop them, every one.	und lass' die Uhren alle, alle steh'n.
And yet, to be afraid of time is useless.	Allein man muss sich auch vor ihr nicht fürchten.
For God, mindful of all his children,	Auch sie ist ein Geschöpf des Vaters,
in his wisdom created it.	der uns alle erschaffen hat.

OCTAVIAN
(tenderly and gently)

My dearest love, why do you torture yourself so with such thoughts?	Mein schöner Schatz, will Sie sich traurig machen mit Gewalt?
Now that I am here,	Wo Sie mich da hat,
and my loving fingers are clasping yours so tenderly,	wo ich meine Finger in Ihre Finger schlinge,
and my eyes look into yours to find an answer,	wo ich mit meinen Augen Ihre Augen suche,
now that I am here,	wo Sie mich da hat—
at such a time can you feel like this?	gerade da ist Ihr so zu Mut?

MARSCHALLIN
(very serious)

Quinquin, now or tomorrow, surely,	Quinquin, heut' oder morgen geht Er hin
you will go from me, leave me and choose another,	und gibt mich auf um einer andern willen,

(hesitating a little)

who's younger and lovelier than I. [14]	die jünger und schöner ist als ich.

OCTAVIAN

So you are trying now to dismiss me	Willst du mit Worten mich von dir stossen
and do with words what your hands refuse?	weil dir die Hände den Dienst nicht tun?

MARSCHALLIN
(calmly)

The day will come unbidden,	Der Tag kommt ganz von selber.
now or tomorrow it will come,	Heut' oder morgen kommt der Tag,
Octavian.	Octavian.

OCTAVIAN

Not now, nor tomorrow! I love you so.	Nicht heut', nicht morgen: ich hab' dich lieb.
Not now nor tomorrow!	Nicht heut', nicht morgen!
The sun shall not rise, that I swear, on such a day!	Wenn's so einen Tag geben muss, ich denk' ihn nicht.
So dreadful a day!	Solch schrecklichen Tag!
That day shall never come,	Ich will den Tag nicht seh'n.
I cannot bear to think of it.	Ich will den Tag nicht denken.
Why break my heart and yours, Therese?	Was quälst du dich und mich, Theres'?

MARSCHALLIN

Now or tomorrow, if not tomorrow, very soon.	Heut' oder morgen oder den übernächsten Tag.
I would not torture you, my love.	Nicht quälen will ich dich, mein Schatz.
It's truth I'm speaking, it's as true for you as 'tis for me ...	Ich sag', was wahr ist, sag's zu mir so gut als wie zu dir.
Let us then lightly meet our fate;	Leicht will ich's machen dir und mir.
light must we be,	Leicht muss man sein:
with spirits light and gentle fingers	mit leichtem Herz und leichten Händen,
take all our pleasures, take them and leave them.	halten und nehmen, halten und lassen ...
Unless we do much grief awaits us, not even God himself will pity us.	Die nicht so sind, die straft das Leben und Gott erbarmt sich ihrer nicht.

74

OCTAVIAN	
Today you sound like my confessor.	Sie spricht ja heute wie ein Pater.
Do you tell me that I may never, may	Soll das heissen, dass ich Sie nie, nie mehr
never love and kiss you	werde küssen dürfen,
till you are faint with rapture?	bis Ihr der Atem ausgeht?

MARSCHALLIN
(softly)

Quinquin, now you must go. Now you must leave me;	[5, 2] Quinquin, Er soll jetzt geh'n, Er soll mich lassen,
I'll go now, go to church, and pray,	Ich werd' jetzt in die Kirchen geh'n
and later visit my Uncle Greifenklau,	und später fahr' ich zum Onkel Greifenklau,
who's old and so ailing,	der alt und gelähmt ist,
and dine with him: 'twill please the dear old man.	und ess' mit ihm: das freut den alten Mann.
This afternoon I will send to your house a footman,	Und Nachmittag werd' ich Ihm einen Lauffer schicken,
Quinquin, and he will tell you	Quinquin, und sagen lassen,
if I, in the Prater, ride;	ob ich in den Prater fahr'.
and if I do	Und wenn ich fahr'
and should you wish,	und Er hat Lust,
you may meet me in the Prater riding	so wird Er auch in den Prater kommen
and you may ride beside my carriage.	und neben meinem Wagen reiten.
And now be good. Do as I say.	Jetzt sei Er gut und folg' Er mir.

OCTAVIAN
(softly)

As you command, Bichette.	Wie Sie befiehlt, Bichette.

Exit. A pause.

MARSCHALLIN
(Alone. Starting up passionately)

He's gone without even a kiss.	Ich hab' ihn nicht einmal geküsst.

(She rings the bell violently. Footmen hurry in from the right.)

Run, try to stop the Count	Lauft's dem Herrn Grafen nach
and say that I beg for a word with him.	und bittet's ihn noch auf ein Wort herauf.

(The footmen hurry off.)

I have let him go from me, and without a single kiss!	Ich hab' ihn fortgeh'n lassen und ihn nicht einmal geküsst!

She sits down on the chair by the dressing-table. The footmen return out of breath.

FIRST FOOTMAN	
But the Count is off and away.	Der Herr Graf sind auf und davon.
SECOND FOOTMAN	
In a flash he seized the bridle.	Gleich beim Tor sind aufgesessen.
THIRD FOOTMAN	
Swung up in the stirrups.	Reitknecht hat gewartet.
FOURTH FOOTMAN	
At the door he seized the bridle like the wind.	Gleich beim Tor sind aufgesessen wie der Wind.
FIRST FOOTMAN	
Galloped round the corner like the wind.	Waren um die Ecken wie der Wind.
SECOND FOOTMAN	
We hurried after.	Sind nachgelaufen.
THIRD FOOTMAN	
We cried ourselves hoarse.	Wir haben geschrien.
FIRST FOOTMAN	
All in vain.	War umsonst.
THIRD FOOTMAN	
Galloped round the corner like the wind.	Waren um die Ecken wie der Wind.
MARSCHALLIN	
Very well. You may leave me.	Es ist gut, geht nur wieder.

(The footmen withdraw. The Marschallin calls after them.)

Send Mohammed!	Den Mohammed!

(The little Black Boy enters with tinkling bells, as before, and bows.) [9a]

Take this case ...	Das da trag'—
(The Page takes the leather jewel-case eagerly.)	
Wait till I say where. To Count Octavian.	[6] Weisst ja nicht wohin. Zum Grafen Octavian.
Give it and say,	Gib's ab und sag':
within is the silver rose.	Da drinn ist die silberne Ros'n.
He will know what he must do.	Der Herr Graf weiss ohnehin.

The Black Boy runs off. The Marschallin leans her head on her hand, and remains deep in thought until the curtain falls. [1]

The curtain begins to fall slowly and noiselessly, but from the fourth crotchet of the fermata quickly.

Ava June as the Marschallin in the ENO production by John Copley. (photo: Mike Humphrey)

Act Two

A room in Herr von Faninal's house. The central doors lead to an antechamber. Doors to right and left. A large window on the right. Chairs against the wall on either side of the main doors. In the rounded corners on either side are secret doors. A footman stands on either side of the main door. Faninal, Sophie, Marianne Leitmetzerin (her Duenna), the Major-Domo, Footmen. [24, 25, 20, 26]

FANINAL
(on the point of saying good-bye to Sophie)

A solemn day, a wondrous day,	Ein ernster Tag, ein grosser Tag!
a festal day, a sacred day!	Ein Ehrentag, ein heil'ger Tag!

Sophie kisses his hand.

MARIANNE

The new coach is there with our man on the box.	Der Josef fahrt vor, mit der neuen Kaross',
Its curtains are of sky-blue.	hat himmelblaue Vorhäng',
Four shining horses are there.	vier Apfelschimmel sind dran.

MAJOR-DOMO
(confidentially to Faninal)

It's high time now Your Lordship should be leaving.	Ist höchste Zeit, dass Euer Gnaden fahren.
It's customary for the bride's father	Der hochadelige Brautvater,*
to have taken his	sagt die Schicklichkeit,
departure from the house	muss ausgefahren sein,
before the silver Rosenkavalier comes here.	bevor der silberne Rosenkavalier vorfährt.
It were not seemly	Wär' nicht geziemend,
for you to meet him at the palace door.	dass vor der Tür sie sich begegneten.

Footmen open the door.

FANINAL

May Heaven help me. When I come again,	In Gottes Namen. Wenn ich wiederkomm',
I shall be leading your bridegroom-to-be by the hand.	so führ' ich deinen Herrn Zukünftigen bei der Hand.

MARIANNE

The excellent and noble Baron Lerchenau!	Den edlen und gestrengen Herrn von Lerchenau!

(Exit Faninal. Sophie comes forward alone. Marianne is at the window.)

Up go the steps. The footmen one by one are springing up behind.	Jetzt steigt er ein. Der Xaver und der Anton springen hinten auf.
The little page has handed up the whip,	Der Stallpag' reicht dem Josef seine Peitschen.
and there are faces at every house.	Alle Fenster sind voller Leut'.

SOPHIE

In this most wonderful and serious moment,	[29] In dieser feierlichen Stunde der Prüfung,
in which You, my Creator (more than I deserve) have brought me	da du mich, o mein Schöpfer, über mein Verdienst erhöhen
and to allow me to enter my married life	und in den heiligen Ehestand führen willst,

(controlling herself with great difficulty)

I will offer humbly my heart, my heart to him.	opfr' ich dir in Demut mein Herz — in Demut auf.
My flesh is too weak to be humble,	Die Demut in mir zu erwecken,
so I must humble myself.	muss ich mich demütigen.

MARIANNE
(very excited)

And half the town is out of doors.	Die halbe Stadt ist auf die Füss'.
See them in the cloister, the good monks one and all are at the windows	Aus dem Seminari schaun die Hochwürdigen von die Balkoner.
and one old man sits high up upon the roof.	Ein alter Mann sitzt oben auf der Latern'.

---

* Hofmannsthal and the vocal score have 'Brautigamsvater' (i.e. father of the groom) and Clemens Krauss made this alteration in the full score.

(struggling to collect her thoughts)

Humble myself and from temptation, from envy, from sin, from evil thoughts, must always pray to save myself!	Demütigen und recht bedenken: die Sünde, die Schuld, die Niedrigkeit, die Verlassenheit, die Anfechtung!
My mother is dead and I am all alone, here in prayer before Thy throne. Here at the altar with Thy blessing I stand.	Die Mutter ist tot und ich bin ganz allein. Für mich selber steh' ich ein. Aber die Ehe ist ein heiliger Stand.

MARIANNE
(as before)

He comes, he comes with two great coaches.	Er kommt, er kommt in zwei Karossen.
The first one has four horses, it is empty. But the next one has six dapple greys. I can see him, the Rosenkavalier!	Die erste ist vierspännig, die ist leer. In der zweiten, sechsspännigen, sitzt er selber, der Rosenkavalier.

THREE FOOTMEN
(running before Octavian's carriage in the street below)

Rofrano, Rofrano!	Rofrano, Rofrano!

SOPHIE
(almost losing her self-control)

I will not be swollen with pride of station after marriage— —after my marriage.	Ich will mich niemals meines neuen Standes überheben— —mich überheben.

(She can control herself no longer.)

What is it they cry?	Was rufen denn die?

MARIANNE

They call him the Rosenkavalier and cry the names of the noble lords related to your husband, that I hear.	Den Namen vom Rosenkavalier und alle Namen von deiner neuen, fürstlichen Verwandtschaft rufens aus.
Now the servants form a pathway. The outriders are beside the door!	Jetzt rangier'n sich die Bedienten. Die Lakaien springen rückwärts ab!

THREE FOOTMEN
(closer)

Rofrano, Rofrano!	Rofrano, Rofrano!

SOPHIE

Oh, but when my husband comes will everyone run to greet him, and his name and titles too?	Werden sie mein' Bräutigam sein' Namen [2, 26] auch so ausrufen, wenn er angefahren kommt!?

THREE FOOTMEN
(right under the window)

Rofrano, Rofrano!	Rofrano, Rofrano!

MARIANNE
(quite beside herself)

The coach door is open and he comes, all in silver clad, he is glittering from head to foot. Like an archangel all on fire.	Sie reissen den Schlag auf! Er steigt aus! Ganz in Silberstück' ist er angelegt, von Kopf zu Fuss. Wie ein heil'ger Engel schaut er aus.

She hastily shuts the window.

SOPHIE

Merciful Heaven! I know that pride must be a mortal sin. But today never can I humble myself. It's all in vain. I can't help being proud, so proud!	Herrgott im Himmel! Ich weiss, der Stolz ist eine schwere Sünd', aber jetzt kann ich mich nicht demütigen. Jetzt geht's halt nicht! Denn das ist ja so schön, so schön!

Two of Faninal's Footmen quickly open the centre doors. Enter Octavian, bareheaded, dressed all in white and silver, carrying the Silver Rose in his hand. Behind him are his servants in his livery, white and pale green. The Footmen, the Heyducks with their curved Hungarian swords at their side; the Couriers in white leather with green ostrich plumes. Immediately behind Octavian a black servant carrying his hat, and another Footman who carries the case for the Silver Rose in both hands. Behind these, Faninal's servants. Octavian, taking the rose in his right hand, advances with noble grace towards Sophie; but his youthful features bear traces of embarrassment, and he blushes. Sophie turns deathly pale with excitement at his splendid appearance. They stand facing each other, each disconcerted by the confusion and beauty of the other. [26]

OCTAVIAN
(with slight hesitation)

It is an honour, an enchantment	[28] Mir ist die Ehre widerfahren,
to which I'll stay most deeply sensible all my days,	dass ich der hoch- und wohlgeborenen Jungfer Braut,
to come here as messenger at	in meines Herrn Vetters Namen,
my Cousin Lerchenau's bidding,	dessen zu Lerchenau Namen,
to offer you as token of his love this rose.	die Rose seiner Liebe überreichen darf.

SOPHIE
(taking the rose)

I am to Your Honour much indebted.	Ich bin Euer Liebden sehr verbunden.
I am to Your Honour to all Eternity indebted.	Ich bin Euer Liebden in aller Ewigkeit verbunden.

(momentary confusion; she smells the rose)

There is a scent in its petals of roses, like the living ones!	Hat einen starken Geruch wie Rosen, wie lebendige!

OCTAVIAN

Yes, there's a drop of oil of Persian roses in its heart.	Ja, ist ein Tropfen persischen Rosenöls darein getan.

SOPHIE

Like heavenly, not earthly flowers, like roses	Wie himmlische, nicht irdische, wie Rosen
from golden gardens of Paradise. Think you not so?	vom hochheiligen Paradies. Ist Ihm nicht auch?

Octavian bends over the rose which she holds out to him, then raises his head and looks at her lips.

It's like a gift from Heaven. Oh, so sweet and rare that no one dare breathe it again.	Ist wie ein Gruss vom Himmel. Ist bereits zu stark, als dass man's ertragen kann.
Drawing me on, as though it were tugging at my heart.	Zieht einen nach, als lägen Stricke um das Herz.

(softly)

Where have I been before and felt such rapture?	[29] Wo war ich schon einmal und war so selig?

OCTAVIAN
(at the same time, as though unconscious, and still more softly)

Where have I been before and felt such rapture?	Wo war ich schon einmal und war so selig?

SOPHIE
(with deep expression)

To walk those blessed fields of Paradise once more. I fear not death itself.	Dahin muss ich zurück! und müsst' ich völlig sterben auf dem Weg.
And yet why dream of death?	Allein, ich sterb' ja nicht.
It's far, it's far, it's an eternity	Das ist ja weit. Ist Zeit und Ewigkeit
that shines on moments of blessedness,	in einem sel'gen Augenblick,
never to be forgotten till death close my eyes.	den will ich nie vergessen bis an meinen Tod.

OCTAVIAN
(at the same time)

I was a child,	Ich war ein Bub,
I never heard her voice until today.	da hab' ich die noch nicht gekannt.
But who am I?	Wer bin denn ich?
What fate brings me to her?	Wie komm' denn ich zu ihr?
What fate brings her to me?	Wie kommt denn sie zu mir?
Feeling and sense would leave me, were I not a man;	Wär' ich kein Mann, die Sinne möchten mir vergeh'n.
this is a moment of blessedness,	Das ist ein sel'ger Augenblick,
never to be forgotten till death close my eyes.	den will ich nie vergessen bis an meinen Tod.

In the meantime Octavian's servants have taken up their positions on the left at the back, Faninal's servants with the Major-Domo to the right. Octavian's Footman hands the jewel-case to Marianne. Sophie wakes from her reverie and gives the rose to Marianne, who places it in the jewel-case. The Footman with the hat approaches Octavian and gives it to him. Octavian's servants withdraw, and at the same time Faninal's servants carry three chairs to the centre, two for Sophie and Octavian, and one for Marianne, further back and to one side. Faninal's Major-Domo carries the jewel-case with the rose through the door to the right, the other servants immediately withdraw through the centre doors. Sophie and Octavian stand facing each other, partly restored to the everyday world, but a little embarrassed. At a signal from Sophie both seat themselves, and the Duenna does likewise, at the same moment as the door on the right is locked from the outside by the Major-Domo.

SOPHIE

I know you very well, mon cousin! [30] Ich kenn' Ihn schon recht wohl, mon cousin!

OCTAVIAN

You know me, ma cousine? Sie kennt mich, ma cousine?

SOPHIE

Yes, and I've read in the court almanac too, Ja, aus dem Buch, wo die Stammbäumer drin sind.
'The Mirror of Nobility'. Dem Ehrenspiegel Österreichs.
I take it every evening up to bed Das nehm' ich immer abends mit ins Bett
and read about the Princes and Dukes, und such' mir meine zukünft'ge gräflich'
and the Counts who will soon be my relations. und fürstlich' Verwandtschaft d'rin zusammen.

OCTAVIAN

Do you so, ma cousine? Tut Sie das, ma cousine?

SOPHIE

I know how old Your Lordship is: Ich weiss, wie alt Euer Liebden sind:
seventeen and a quarter. Siebzehn Jahr' und zwei Monat'.
I know all your firstnames too: Octavian, Maria Ehrenreich, Ich weiss all' Ihre Taufnamen: Octavian Maria Ehrenreich
Bonaventura, Fernand, Hyacinth. Bonaventura Fernand Hyacinth.

OCTAVIAN

I do not know them even half as well. So gut weiss ich sie selber nicht einmal.

SOPHIE

I know also . . . Ich weiss noch was.
She blushes.

OCTAVIAN

What do you know, tell me pray, ma cousine? Was weiss Sie noch, sag' Sie mir's, ma cousine?

SOPHIE
(not looking at him)
Quinquin. Quinquin.

OCTAVIAN
(laughing)
So you know that name too? Weiss Sie den Namen auch?

SOPHIE

Men call you Quinquin when they have your friendship, So nennen Ihn halt Seine guten Freunde
and lovely ladies, I suppose, und schöne Damen, denk' ich mir,
with whom you are acquainted. mit denen Er recht gut ist.
(slight pause; naively)
I'm happy I'll marry soon! Will you not like it too? Ich freu' mich aufs Heiraten! Freut Er sich auch darauf?
But perhaps you have not given thought to it, mon cousin? Oder hat Er leicht noch gar nicht dran gedacht, mon cousin?
You think, it is another matter happy and free. Denk' Er: Ist doch was andres als der ledige Stand.

OCTAVIAN
(softly, as she speaks)
What charm she has! Wie schön sie ist.

SOPHIE

But then you are a man, and men are what they are.	Freilich, Er ist ein Mann, da ist Er, was Er bleibt.
I'll need a husband all my days, to guide my steps;	Ich aber brauch' erst einen Mann, dass ich was bin.
and I'll show him my thanks by doing what he tells me.	Dafür bin ich dem Mann dann auch gar sehr verschuldet.

OCTAVIAN
(deeply moved and softly)

My God, how good and fair she is.	Mein Gott, wie schön und gut sie ist.
She makes me quite confused.	Sie macht mich ganz verwirrt.

SOPHIE

I never shall disgrace him, never	Ich werd' ihm keine Schand' nicht machen—
forget my rank and station.	und meinem Rang und Vortritt.
Should another wife look down her nose at me	Täte eine, die sich besser dünkt als ich,
or go before me	ihn mir bestreiten
at a Christening or a funeral,	bei einer Kindstauf' oder Leich',
I'll show her very quickly,	so will ich, wenn es sein muss,
if needs must be with a slapped cheek,	mit Ohrfeigen ihr beweisen,
that I am finer bred than she,	dass ich die vornehmere bin
and I'll bear anything rather	und lieber alles hinnehme
than vulgar pride or insolence!	wie Kränkung oder Ungebühr.

OCTAVIAN
(eagerly)

Ah, do but name the wretch	Wie kann Sie denn nur denken,
who would presume to hazard such impertinence.	dass man Ihr mit Ungebühr begegnen wird,
For always you'll be the loveliest of all the loveliest creatures.	da Sie doch immer die Schönste, die Allerschönste sein wird?

SOPHIE

Why do you laugh, mon cousin?	Lacht Er mich aus, mon cousin?

OCTAVIAN

What? And why should I laugh?	Wie, glaubt Sie das von mir?

SOPHIE

You are allowed to laugh, if you will.	Er darf mich auslachen, wenn Er will.
From you I will gladly take all that you choose,	Von Ihm lass' ich alles mir gerne gescheh'n,
for I tell you, no gentleman of all I've met with,	weil mir nie noch ein junger Kavalier
no, nor dreamed of, has so stolen my heart away as you.	von Nähen oder Weitem also wohlgefallen hat wie Er.
Ah, here he comes. It's my bridegroom-to-be.	Jetzt aber kommt mein Herr Zukünftiger.

The door at the back is thrown open. All three rise and step to the right. Faninal ceremoniously conducts the Baron over the threshold towards Sophie, giving him precedence. Lerchenau's servants follow in his footsteps, first the Almoner, then the Body-Servant. Next comes the Huntsman, with another clownish bumpkin, who has a plaster over his battered nose, and two others, no less uncouth, looking as if they had stepped straight from the turnip-fields into their liveries. All, like their master, carry sprigs of myrtle. Faninal's servants remain in the background. [25]

FANINAL

May I present now to Your Lordship? This is your bride-to-be?	Ich präsentiere Euer Gnaden Dero Zukünftige.

BARON
(bowing, then to Faninal)

Delicious! My compliments to you.	Deliziös! Mach' Ihm mein Kompliment.

(He kisses Sophie's hand, as if examining it.)

The wrist is delicate, that's a very good sign.	Ein feines Handgelenk. Darauf halt' ich gar viel.
Among the middle classes it is seldom to be found.	Ist unter Bürgerlichen eine selt'ne Distinktion.

(in an undertone)

My blood runs hots and cold.   Es wird mir heiss und kalt.

FANINAL

Allow me, this is my devoted servant   Gestatten, dass ich die getreue Jungfer
Marianne Leitmetzerin . . .   Marianne Leitmetzerin . . .

He presents Marianne, who curtsies deeply three times.

BARON
(with a gesture of vexation)

Some other time.   Lass' Er das weg.
Come on, I'll introduce you to my   Begrüss' Er jetzt mit mir meinen Herrn
Rosenkavalier.   Rosenkavalier.

*He goes with Faninal towards Octavian, and bows. Octavian returns the bow. Lerchenau's servants
nearly knock Sophie down, come to a standstill, and retire a couple of paces backwards to the
right.*

SOPHIE
(standing on the right with Marianne, in an undertone)

How vulgar his behaviour, he is like a   Was sind das für Manieren? Ist da leicht
  horse-dealer   ein Rosstauscher
who thinks he's bought me at a country   und kommt ihm vor, er hätt' mich
  fair.   eingetauscht?

MARIANNE
(aside)

A cavalier is always unaffected and   Ein Kavalier hat halt ein ungezwungenes,
  easy in his behaviour,   leutseliges Betragen.
tell yourself who he is,   Sag' dir vor, wer er ist
and the rank you will gain,   und zu was er dich macht,
and soon you will forget your silly ways.   so werden dir die Faxen gleich vergeh'n.

BARON
(during the foregoing, to Faninal)

It's quite astounding how the young Count   Ist gar zum Staunen, wie der junge Herr
  resembles someone whom I know.   jemand gewissem ähnlich sieht.
He has a sister, she's a sweet little bastard.   Hat ein Bastardel, recht ein saub'res zur
     Schwester.
It is no secret round the Imperial court.   Ist kein Geheimnis unter Personen von
     Stand.
Her Highness told me so herself.   Hab's aus der Fürstin eig'nem Mund
(genially)
And since our Faninal, now that he's   und weil der Faninal sozusagen jetzo
  ennobled,
is one of us in a way   zu der Verwandtschaft gehört,
do not be ashamed, my dear Rofrano,   mach' dir kein Dépit darum Rofrano,
that your father has sowed his wild oats;   dass dein Vater ein Streichmacher war,
he's not the only one who's had some on   befindet sich dabei in guter Kompagnie,
  the side, the honourable Marchese.   der sel'ge Herr Marchese.
I get around a bit myself.   Ich selber exkludier' mich nicht.
(to Faninal)
Look well now at that long-legged rascal   Seh', Liebden, schau dir dort den Langen
  there,   an,
the fair one, at the back.   den blonden, hinten dort.
I cannot point my finger at him,   Ich will ihn nicht mit Fingern weisen,
but you will see at a glance   aber er sticht wohl hervor,
how he's distinguished by his high-born   durch eine adelige Contenance.
  features.
Is he not truly a splendid fellow?   Ist aber ein ganz besond'rer Kerl.
He has a noble pedigree   Sagt nichts, weil ich der Vater bin,
but he's the greatest fool of all my   hat's aber faustdick hinter den Ohren.
  household.

SOPHIE
(during the above)

What breeding's this to leave me standing   Jetzt lässt er mich so steh'n, der grobe
  here?   Ding!

And he is my husband that's to be.
And pock-marked also is his face, on my soul!

Und das ist mein Zukünftiger.
Und blattersteppig ist er auch, o mein Gott!

MARIANNE

Well, if his front displeases you so, young Mistress Haughty,
then from the back regard him well,
and then you'll find something that is good to see.

Na, wenn er dir von vorn nicht gefallt, du Jungfer Hochmut,
so schau ihn dir von rückwärts an,
da wirst was seh'n, was dir schon gefallen wird.

SOPHIE

Then tell me what it is that I shall find.

Möcht' wissen, was ich da schon sehen werd'.

MARIANNE
(mimicking her)

Then tell me what it is that I shall find.

Möcht' wissen, was ich da schon sehen werd'.

Why, that your patron saints have sent you this day
one of Her Majesty's
High Chamberlains as bridegroom.
That is very clear to see.

Dass es ein kaiserlicher Kämmerer ist,
den dir dein Schutzpatron
als Herrn Gemahl spendiert hat.
Das kannst sehn mit einem Blick.

The Major-Domo approaches Lerchenau's servants most politely and conducts them out of the room. At the same time Faninal's servants withdraw, except for two, who offer round wine and confits.

FANINAL
(to the Baron)

I wonder if you'd like! It's a very old brandy.

Belieben jetzt vielleicht?—ist ein alter Tokaier.

Octavian and the Baron serve themselves.

BARON

Good Faninal, you know what's right and fit,
to serve such a fine old brandy to toast a fine young daughter.
You've done this not too badly.

Brav Faninal, Er weiss was sich gehört.
Serviert einen alten Tokaier zu einem jungen Mädel.
Ich bin mit Ihm zufrieden.

(to Octavian)

With two-a-penny nobles like this one, we must show them
that they are not our equals, you understand me.
Persons like us have a duty to condescend.

Musst denen Bagatelladeligen immer zeigen,
dass nicht für unsresgleichen sich anseh'n dürfen,
muss immer was von Herablassung dabei sein.

OCTAVIAN
(pointedly)

I'm all admiration for Your Lordship!
Your Lordship's manners are so subtle.
You should be sent as an ambassador all over Europe.

Ich muss Deine Liebden sehr bewundern.
Hast wahrhaft grosse Weltmanieren.
Könnt'st einen Ambassadeur vorstellen heut oder morgen.

BARON
(roughly)

I'll bring her over for a chat.
See if they've taught her to speak properly.
I'll soon discover if she's well informed.

Ich hol' mir jetzt das Mädel her.
Soll uns jetzt Konversation vormachen,
damit ich seh', wie sie beschlagen ist.

He takes Sophie by the hand, and leads her back with him.

Eh bien! Now, talk to us a while,
me and my cousin Tavvy,
Say, to begin with, what do you fancy will please you most as a bride?

Eh bien! nun plauder Sie uns eins,
mir und dem Vetter Taverl!
Sag' Sie heraus, auf was Sie sich halt in der Eh' am meisten freut!

The Baron seats himself and tries to make her sit on his lap.

SOPHIE
(pulling away from him)

What do you mean?

Wo denkt Er hin?

BARON
(at his ease)

Pah! What do I mean? Let me whisper in your ear.
And I will tell you frankly just what I mean.

Pah! Wo ich hindenk? Komm Sie da ganz nah zu mir,
dann will ich Ihr erzählen, wo ich hindenk.

Same business. Sophie pulls more angrily away from him.

BARON
(at his ease)

Would my lady prefer it if I were to play

the dancing-master, bowing and cavorting?
With 'mille pardons' and 'devotion',
and 'By your leave', and 'My respects'?

Wär Ihr leicht präferabel, dass man gegen Ihrer

den Zeremonienmeister sollt hervortun?
Mit 'mill pardon' und 'Devotion',
und 'Geh da weg' und 'hab Respeckt'?

SOPHIE

Undoubtedly, yes, would surely be much better!

Wahrhaftig und ja gefiele mir das besser!

BARON
(laughing)

Not for me! I tell you! None of that for me, miss!
I am an open-hearted country lad, I like a free and easy life.

Mir auch nicht! Da sieht Sie! Mir auch ganz und gar nicht!
Bin einer biedern offenherzigen Galanterie recht zugetan.

He starts to kiss her, but she energetically pushes him away.

FANINAL
(offering Octavian the second chair, which he refuses)

How can it be? There sits a Lerchenau
and sets his heart upon our little Sophie, the rascals might be man and wife.
And there stands a Rofrano, makes as if at home—
a Count Rofrano, nothing less,
and brother to Her Majesty's Lord High Rod.

Wie ist mir denn! Da sitzt ein Lerchenau
und karessiert in Ehrbarkeit mein Sopherl,
als wär' sie ihm schon angetraut.
Und da steht ein Rofrano, grad' als müsst's so sein—
ein Graf Rofrano, sonsten nix—
der Bruder vom Marchese Obersttruchsess.

OCTAVIAN
(angrily, aside)

There's a rude fellow. There's nothing I'd like better
than once to catch him
sword in hand and no one to watch.
No, nothing better in the world.

Das ist ein Kerl, dem möcht' ich wo begegnen
mit meinem Degen da,
wo ihn kein Wächter schreien hört.
Ja, das ist alles, was ich möcht'.

SOPHIE
(to the Baron)

Let go of me. You're not my husband!

Ei lass Er doch, wir sind nicht so vertraut!

BARON
(to Sophie)

No need to be shy before Cousin Tavvy!

Don't be so modest. Why, you know in Paris,
where they have the very finest manners, newly weds,
doing the things that newly weds like to do,
send invitations out to assorted friends
to watch them. Yes, to the King's invited . . .

Geniert Sie sich leicht vor dem Vetter Taverl?

Da hat Sie Unrecht. Hör' Sie, in Paris,
wo doch die Hohe Schul' ist für Manieren, gibt's frei nichts
was unter jungen Eheleuten geschieht
wozu man nicht Einladungen liess' ergeh'n
zum Zuschau'n, ja an den König selber.

FANINAL
(aside)

Would that my palace were of glass,
every pettifogging merchant in the town,

jaundiced with envy should see them sit *en famille*.
For that pleasure I'd give my richest house right gladly, 'pon my soul.

Wär nur die Mauer da von Glas,
dass alle bürgerlichen Neidhammeln von Wien

sie en famille beisammen so sitzen seh'n!
Dafür wollt ich mein Lerchenfelder Eckhaus geben, meiner Seel'!

OCTAVIAN
(furious)

How can I bear to watch him there, so coarse, it's unforgivable. Would I could fly away from here!	Dass ich das Mannsbild sehen muss, so frech, so unverschämt mit ihr. Könnt' ich hinaus und fort von hier!

The Baron grows more and more importunate; Sophie is at her wits' end.

BARON
(to Sophie)

Don't be so silly now, for you belong to me!	Lass Sie die Flausen nur: gehört doch jetzo mir!
It's all right. Now be good! It all works like a charm.	Geht all's recht! Sei Sie gut. Geht all's so wie am Schnürl!

(half to himself, fondling her)

Just as I like it! Tender as a chicken!	Ganz meine Massen! Schultern wie ein Henderl!
Thin as a rake—no matter. But so white,	Hundsmager noch—das macht nichts, aber weiss
white as driven snow. There's nothing I like more!	mit einem Glanz, wie ich ihn ästimier!
I have the luck of all the Lerchenaus!	Ich hab' halt ja ein Lerchenauisch Glück!

(Sophie tears herself away and stamps her foot.)
(delighted)

Gad! She's a fine little peppery spitfire!	Ist Sie ein rechter Kaprizenschädel!

(rises and runs after her)

And see how hot her cheeks are burning, hot enough to burn your hands!	Steigt Ihr das Blut gar in die Wangen, dass man sich die Hand verbrennt?

SOPHIE
(flushing with anger)

Just take your hands from me!	Lass' Er die Hand davon!

Octavian in silent anger, crushes the glass he holds in his hand, and throws the pieces to the ground.

MARIANNE

(She runs with affected grace towards Octavian, picks up the pieces, and confides her delight to him.)

He has uncommon easy ways, the Herr Baron!	Ist recht ein familiärer Mann, der Herr Baron!
He's quite enchanting, such originality!	Man delektiert sich, was er all's für Einfälle hat!

BARON
(near Sophie)

Nothing suits me better.	Geht mir nichts darüber!
No kind of simperings or tender airs could give me half such pleasure, on my soul!	Könnt' mich mit Schmachterei und Zärtlichkeit nicht halb so glücklich machen, meiner Seel!

SOPHIE
(furious, to his face)

I do not care if I please you or not!	Ich denk nicht d'ran, dass ich Ihn glücklich mach'!

BARON
(complacently)

You please me fine, no matter if you like it or you don't.	Sie wird es tun, ob Sie daran wird denken oder nicht.

OCTAVIAN
(aside, pale with anger)

Away! Away, without farewell! Or else I cannot tell just what I might be led to do! No longer can I stay here! I must go!	Hinaus! Hinaus! und kein Adieu! Sonst steh' ich nicht dafür, dass ich nicht was Verwirrtes tu! Hinaus aus diesen Stuben! Nur hinaus!

In the meantime the Notary has entered with the Clerk, introduced by Faninal's Major-Domo. He announces them in a whisper to Faninal. Faninal goes towards the Notary at the back, speaks to him, and looks through a bundle of documents which the Clerk presents to him.

SOPHIE
(between her teeth)

There is no man has ever dared to speak to me like this.	Hat nie kein Mann dergleichen Reden nicht zu mir geführt!
What can you think of me, and yourself?	Möcht wissen, was Ihm dünkt von mir und Ihm?
What are you, sir, to me?	Was ist Er denn zu mir?

BARON
(contentedly)

You'll find out overnight,	Wird kommen über Nacht,
with sweetest joy	dass Sie ganz sanft
you'll learn just what I am to you.	wird wissen, was ich bin zu Ihr.
Just like the little song—you surely know it?	Ganz wie's im Liedel heisst—kennt Sie das Liedel?
'Lalalalala— [31]	'Lalalalala—

(very sentimentally)

My love shall be your all in all!	wie ich dein Alles werde sein!
With me, with me you will find no room too small,	Mit mir, mit mir keine Kammer dir zu klein,
without me, without me, lonely days feel so wrong,	ohne mich, ohne mich jeder Tag dir so bang,

(impudently and coarsely)

with me, with me nights cannot be too long.'	[32] mit mir, mit mir keine Nacht dir zu lang!'

As he tries to draw Sophie still closer to him, she frees herself, and violently pushes him back.

MARIANNE
(hurrying to Sophie)

He has uncommon easy ways, the Herr Baron!	Ist recht ein familiärer Mann, der Herr Baron!
He's quite enchanting, such originality!	Man delektiert sich, was er all's für Einfäll' hat,

(nervously and excitedly)

Such originality, the Herr Baron!	was er all's für Einfäll' hat, der Herr Baron!

OCTAVIAN
(without looking, and yet aware of all that is going on)

It's more than I can stomach!	Ich steh auf glüh'nden Kohlen!
I stand on coals of fire!	Ich fahr' aus meiner Haut!
I'm doing penance in an hour	Ich büss' in dieser einen Stund
for many years of sin!	all meine Sünden ab!

BARON
(aside, very contented)

I always did say, I have all the luck [33] of the Lerchenaus.	Wahrhaftig und ja, ich hab' halt ein Lerchenauisch Glück!
Nothing else in the world so inflames my desire	Gibt gar nichts auf der Welt, was mich so enflammiert
or so invigorates my soul like a defiant wench.	und also vehement verjüngt als wie ein rechter Trotz!

(Faninal and the Notary, followed by the Clerk, have advanced to the front left of the stage. As soon as he sees the Notary, the Baron addresses Sophie eagerly, without the slightest idea what she is thinking.)

But now there's work to do: you must do without me.	Doch gibt's Geschäfter jetzt, muss mich dispensieren,
They need my help in there.	bin dort von Wichtigkeit. Indessen
And meanwhile there's cousin Tavvy, he will entertain you!	der Vetter Taverl leistet Ihr Gesellschaft!

FANINAL

If it's now convenient, dear son-in-law?	Wenn es jetzt belieben tät, Herr Schwiegersohn!

BARON
(eagerly)

Of course it is convenient.	Natürlich wird's belieben.

(in passing, to Octavian, touching him familiarly)

I've no objection,	Hab nichts dawider,
if you would like to flirt a little, cousin,	wenn du ihr möchtest Äugerl machen, Vetter,
now or at any time.	jetzt oder künftighin.
She's still in need of breaking in.	Ist noch ein rechter Rühr-nicht-an.
The more she learns from you, the better it will please me.	Betrachts als förderlich, je mehr sie degourdiert wird.
She is just like a filly, still unsaddled and shy.	Ist wie bei einem jungen ungerittenen Pferd.
The husband in the end gets everything he wants,	Kommt alls dem Angetrauten letzterdings zu Gut',
so long as he's wise enough to exercise his matrimonial rights.	wofern er sein eh'lich Privilegium zu Nutz zu machen weiss.

The Baron goes to the left. The servant who had admitted the Notary has in the meantime opened the door on the left. Faninal and the Notary make for the door. The Baron fixes his eye on Faninal, and indicates to him that he must keep a distance of three paces. Faninal obsequiously retreats. The Baron takes precedence, assures himself that Faninal is three paces behind him, and walks solemnly through the door on the left. Faninal follows, and after him come the Notary and his Clerk. The Footman closes the door on the left, and goes out, leaving the door leading to the anteroom open. The Footman who was serving refreshments has retired. Sophie stands on the right, confused and humiliated. Marianne curtsies in the direction of the door until it closes. Octavian, quivering with excitement, hurries over to Sophie, glancing back to make sure the others have gone.

OCTAVIAN

And will you marry that bumpkin, ma cousine?	Wird Sie das Mannsbild da heiraten, ma cousine?

SOPHIE
(taking a step towards him, in a whisper)

Not for the world!	Nicht um die Welt!

(glancing at her Duenna)

Oh, God! Could we but be alone, that I might beg of you, that I might beg of you!	Mein Gott, wär ich allein mit Ihm, dass ich Ihn bitten könnt! dass ich Ihn bitten könnt!

OCTAVIAN
(quickly, in an undertone)

What is it you would beg of me? Tell me now, quick!	Was ist's, dass Sie mich bitten möcht'? Sag' Sie mir's schnell!

SOPHIE
(taking another step towards him)

Oh my God, I would ask your help! And you cannot help me because he is your cousin Lerchenau.	O mein Gott, dass Er mir halt hilft! Und Er wird mir nicht helfen wollen, weil es halt Sein Vetter ist!

OCTAVIAN
(vehemently)

He is cousin by courtesy; praised be God above, I never saw him in my life until this time yesterday.	Nenn ihn Vetter aus Höflichkeit; Gott sei Lob und Dank, hab' ihn im Leben vor dem gestrigen Tage nie geseh'n!

Some of the servant girls rush headlong across the anteroom hotly pursued by Lerchenau's attendants. The Body-Servant and the servant with the plaster on his nose are at the heels of a pretty young girl, and corner her close by the salon door.

FANINAL'S MAJOR-DOMO
(running in much perturbed, calling the Duenna to help him)

His Lordship's servants, drunk as a lord, if you please, ma'am, are scaring our girls to death, twenty times worse than the Turks, ma'am, or Croatians.	Die Lerchenau'schen sind voller Brannt-wein gesoffen und gehn aufs Gesinde los, zwanzigmal ärger als Türken und Croaten!

MARIANNE

Fetch up our people to help you, where can they be?	Hol Er von unseren Leuten, wo sind denn die?

She runs off with the Major-Domo. They rescue the girl from her assailants and lead her away. All disappear. The anteroom remains empty.

SOPHIE
(speaking freely now that she is unobserved)

My trust is in your kindness, mon cousin,	[34] Zu Ihm hätt' ich ein Zutrau'n, mon cousin,
kindness like no one's in the world.	so wie zu niemand auf der Welt,
Ah, you could be my saviour,	dass Er mir könnte helfen,
if you only had the will to be!	wenn Er nur den guten Willen hätt'!

OCTAVIAN

First you must yourself take courage,	Erst muss Sie sich selber helfen,
then I too will help:	dann hilf ich Ihr auch.
till you do that yourself	Tu' Sie das erst für sich,
there is naught I can do.	dann tu' ich was für Sie!

SOPHIE
(confidingly, almost tenderly)

What do you mean, what is it I must do?   Was ist denn das, was ich zuerst muss tun?

OCTAVIAN
(softly)

You know that already!   Das wird Sie wohl wissen!

SOPHIE
(looking at him undismayed)

And what is it that you will do for me?	Und was ist das, was Er für mich will tun,
Ah, tell me pray!	nun sag' Er mir's!

OCTAVIAN
(with determination)

Now you must stand alone and fight for us both!	Nun muss Sie ganz allein für uns zwei einsteh'n!

SOPHIE

What? For us both?	Wie? Für uns zwei?
Oh, say that again!	O sag' Er's noch einmal.

OCTAVIAN
(softly)

For us both!   Für uns zwei!

SOPHIE
(rapturously)

In all my life I have never heard such words!   Ich hab' im Leben so was Schönes nicht gehört!

OCTAVIAN
(louder)

For you and me you must be steadfast and still be—	Für sich und mich muss Sie sich wehren und bleiben—

SOPHIE

Still be?   Bleiben?

OCTAVIAN

What you are.   Was Sie ist.

(Sophie takes his hand, bends over it, and kisses it quickly before he can withdraw it. He kisses her on the lips and holds her as she nestles up to him; tenderly) *

With eyes all veiled by your tears	[35] Mit Ihren Augen voll Tränen
you're asking my aid, your fears have pierced my heart.	kommt Sie zu mir, damit Sie sich beklagt,
Be brave! Nothing shall touch or hurt you,	vor Angst muss Sie an mich sich lehnen,
your tender heart is full of fear.	Ihr armes Herz ist ganz verzagt.
Now I must find a way to make you trust me,	Und ich muss jetzt als Ihren Freund mich zeigen
and yet I know not how!	und weiss noch gar nicht, wie!
Rapture so blessed, so wondrous	Mir ist so selig, so eigen,
to hold you here in my arms.	dass ich Dich halten darf:
Give answer, but only with silence:	Gib Antwort, aber gib sie mit Schweigen:

---

* See title page note.

did you come of your own free will to find me?	Bist Du von selber so zu mir gekommen?
Say yes or no. Say yes or no.	Ja oder nein? Ja oder nein?
You cannot find the words to tell it.	Du musst es nicht mit Worten sagen—
Say, was it done from choice?	hast Du es gern getan?
Say, was it just your need?	Sag', oder nur aus Not?
Just your need that bade you offer me such marvels,	Nur aus Not so alles zu mir hergetragen,
your heart, your lovely, lovely face?	Dein Herz, Dein liebliches Gesicht?
Say, can it be that long ago	Sag', ist Dir nicht, dass irgendwo
in some divine remembered dream,	in irgend einem schönen Traum
we lived this hour before?	das einmal schon so war?
Think you not so?	Spürst Du's wie ich?
Say, think you not as I?	Sag': spürst Du's so wie ich?
My heart and soul by your side staying,	Mein Herz und Seel' wird bei Ihr bleiben,
whereso'er you are,	wo Sie geht und steht,
for all eternity.	bis in alle Ewigkeit.

SOPHIE

What rapture! Your strongs arms enfold me	Ich möchte mich bei Ihm verstecken
and hide me for ever from the world.	und nichts mehr wissen von der Welt.
When I can feel your heart so close to mine,	Wenn Er mich so in Seinen Armen hält,
nothing in this life is harsh or dreadful.	kann mich nichts Hässliches erschrecken.
I want to stay there, stay	Da bleiben möcht' ich, da!
in silence, and let what may befall,	und schweigen und, was mir auch gescheh',
deep hidden like a linnet in the branches,	geborgen wie der Vogel in den Zweigen
breathless beside you!	stillsteh'n und spüren:
You, you are close at hand!	Er, Er ist in der Näh'!
My heart should fail me now for fear and grief,	Mir müsste angst und bang im Herzen sein,
but no, I feel only joy and blessedness	statt dessen fühl' ich nur Freud' und Seligkeit
and nothing more,	und keine Pein,
I cannot find the words to tell it!	ich könnt' es nicht mit Worten sagen!
Have I been sinful in what I did?	Hab ich was Unrechtes getan?
I sought you in my need!	Ich war halt in der Not!
Your arms were so near!	Da war Er mir nah!
I looked upon your face,	Da war es Sein Gesicht,
your eyes, your manly grace	Sein Auge jung und licht,
and then I knew my place	auf das ich mich gericht'—
was at hand by your side;	Sein liebes Gesicht—
since that moment I know not	und seitdem weiss ich halt nichts—
what I feel any more.	nichts mehr von mir.
Stay, stay close to me,	Bleib' Du nur bei mir.
protect me, save me, stay beside me,	Er muss mir Seinen Schutz vergönnen,
I follow where'er you guide me,	was Er will, werd' ich können:
save me, leave me not.	bleib' nur Er bei mir!
Protect me now and stay beside me,	Er muss mir Seinen Schutz vergönnen,
with your protective arms around me—	was Er wird wollen, werd' ich können—
stay near me, stay ever close by my side.	bleib' Er nur bei mir.

From the secret doors in the rear corners Valzacchi and Annina emerge noiselessly, and watch the lovers. They approach silently on tiptoe. Octavian draws Sophie to him to kiss her; by this time the Italians are right behind them. They duck behind the armchairs. Then they rush out from their hiding-places. Annina seizes Sophie, Valzacchi takes hold of Octavian.

VALZACCHI AND ANNINA
(screaming)

Herr Baron von Lerchenau!—Herr Baron von Lerchenau!	Herr Baron von Lerchenau!—Herr Baron von Lerchenau!

Octavian starts aside to the right.

VALZACCHI
(holding him with difficulty, breathlessly to Annina)

Run, and fetch de Barone!	Lauf und 'ol' Seine Gnade!
Now at once! I must 'old on tight to him!	Snell, nur snell. Ik muss alten diese 'err!

If I let go of her, she will be off!   Lass ich die Fräulein aus, lauft sie mir weg!

BOTH

Herr Baron von Lerchenau,	Herr Baron von Lerchenau!
Herr Baron von Lerchenau!	Herr Baron von Lerchenau!
Come and see your bride-to-be	Komm' zu seh'n die Fräulein Braut!
beside her Rosenkavalier!	Mit eine junge Kavalier!
Come here quickly, come here quickly!	Kommen eilig, kommen hier! Ecco!
Ecco!	

The Baron enters from the left, the Italians let their victims go, spring aside, bow low to the Baron with significant gestures. The Baron with folded arms contemplates the group. Ominous pause. Sophie nestles timidly up to Octavian.

BARON

Eh bien, Mamsell, what have you got to tell me?	Eh bien, Mamsell, was hat Sie mir zu sagen?

(Sophie says nothing. The Baron shows no signs of losing his composure.)

Well, do not hesitate!   Nun, resolvier Sie sich!

SOPHIE

Oh God, what can I tell you?	Mein Gott, was soll ich sagen:
You would not understand!	Er wird mich nicht versteh'n!

BARON
(genially)

I'll be the judge of that.   Das werden wir ja seh'n!

OCTAVIAN
(taking a step nearer to the Baron)

It's my duty to inform Your Lordship	Euer Liebden muss ich halt vermelden,
a most essential change has taken place	dass sich in Seiner Angelegenheit
concerning Mistress Faninal.	was Wichtiges verändert hat.

BARON
(genially)

Oh essential? Change? None that I know!   Verändert? Ei, nicht dass ich wüsst'!

OCTAVIAN

And therefore I now have to tell you!	Darum soll Er es jetzt erfahren!
The lady—	Die Fräulein—

BARON

Heh! You waste no time. You've learned to take your chances	Ei, Er ist nicht faul! Er weiss zu profitieren,
tho' only seventeen, I must congratulate you!	mit Seinen siebzehn Jahr'! Ich muss Ihm gratulieren!

OCTAVIAN

The lady—   Die Fräulein—

BARON
(half to himself)

I was just the same when I was your age,	Ist mir ordentlich, ich seh' mich selber!
you rascal! How you make me laugh, you poodle-puppy!	Muss lachen über den Filou, den pudeljungen.

OCTAVIAN

The lady—   Die Fräulein—

BARON

She's dumb, I presume, and so she's chosen you	Ei! Sie ist wohl stumm und hat Ihn angestellt
to speak as her attorney!	für ihren Advokaten!

OCTAVIAN

The lady—   Die Fräulein—

He breaks off once more, as if to allow Sophie to speak.

SOPHIE
(terrorstruck)

No! No! I cannot say the word.	Nein! Nein! Ich bring' den Mund nicht auf,
You speak for me!	sprech Er für mich!

OCTAVIAN
(with determination)

The lady—

Die Fräulein—

BARON
(mimicking him)

The lady, the lady! The lady!
The lady!
It's like a cheap little circus.
No joking!
So now be off with you before I lose
control.

Die Fräulein, die Fräulein! Die Fräulein!
Die Fräulein!
ist eine Kreuzerkomödi wahrhaftig!

jetzt echappier Er sich, sonst reisst mir
die Geduld.

OCTAVIAN
(very determined)

The lady, in a word,
the lady does not like you.

Die Fräulein, kurz und gut,
die Fräulein mag Ihn nicht.

BARON
(genially)

Never mind about that. She will like what
I teach her.

Sei Er da ausser Sorg'. Wird schon lernen
mich mögen.

(moving towards Sophie)

Come with me to the lawyer, he will
need you soon to sign the marriage
papers.

Komm' Sie da jetzt hinein: wird gleich an
Ihrer sein,
die Unterschrift zu geben.

SOPHIE
(retreating)

No, not for all the world will I go in with
you!
How can a cavalier be so indelicate!

Um keinen Preis geh' ich an Seiner Hand
hinein!
Wie kann ein Kavalier so ohne Zartheit
sein!

OCTAVIAN
(now between the other two and the left-hand door, very emphatically)

It's clear enough! The lady's mind is now
made up;
she says she will let Your Lordship stay
unmarried
for now and evermore.

Versteht Er Deutsch? Die Fräulein hat sich
resolviert,
Sie will Euer Gnaden ungeheirat' lassen

in Zeit und Ewigkeit!

BARON
(with the air of a man in a great hurry)

What nonsense! Poppycock! Your empty
prattle doesn't scare me.
It's time to go!

Mancari! Jungfernred'! ist nicht gehau'n
und nicht gestochen!
Verlaub Sie jetzt!

He takes Sophie by the hand.

OCTAVIAN
(placing himself firmly in front of the door)

If one spark you have in you
of true gentility
then what I just have told you
makes your duty quite clear.

Wenn nur so viel in Ihm ist
von einem Kavalier,
so wird Ihm wohl genügen,
was Er g'hört hat von mir!

BARON
(to Sophie, as if he had not heard)

Thank your lucky stars I choose to close
one eye,
as is correct and seemly for a gentleman!

Gratulier' Sie sich nur, dass ich ein Aug'
zudrück'!
Daran mag Sie erkennen, was ein Kavalier
ist!

He attempts to go past Octavian with her.

OCTAVIAN
(grasping his sword)

There's a way to make my meaning
understood by such as you are!

Wird doch wohl ein Mittel geben,
Seinesgleichen zu bedeuten.

BARON
(not letting go of Sophie, and pushing her towards the door)

That I can scarce believe!

Ei, schwerlich, wüsste nicht!

OCTAVIAN
(losing all self-control)

Of the name of gentleman you are unworthy, sir!	Ich acht' Ihn mit nichten für einen Kavalier!

BARON
(pompously)

Indeed, were I not sure you know what is my due, and were you not a kinsman, I hardly could, I vow, restrain myself from measures of violence!	Wahrhaftig, wüsst' ich nicht, dass Er mich respektiert, und wär' Er nicht verwandt, es wär mir jetzo schwer, dass ich mit Ihm nicht übereinander käm'!

(He attempts with feigned unconcern to lead Sophie towards the centre doors, after the Italians have signalled to him energetically to go that way.)

Come on! Come to your dear beloved father;	Komm' Sie! Geh'n zum Herrn Vater dort hinüber!
we shall find him waiting in there!	Ist bereits der nähere Weg!

OCTAVIAN
(following him, close to Sophie)

I trust you don't forget you've a name to defend.	Ich hoff', Er kommt vielmehr jetzt mit mir hinters Haus,
I know a most convenient garden.	ist dort ein recht bequemer Garten.

BARON
(continuing in the same direction, feigning unconcern, trying to lead Sophie away, and still holding her by the hand. Over his shoulder.)

Another time, it's not convenient now.	Bewahre, wär mir jetzo nicht genehm.
The attorney must not be kept waiting.	Lass um alls den Notari nicht warten.
Would be an affront to my little bride.	Wär' gar ein Affront für die Jungfer Braut!

OCTAVIAN
(pulling his coat sleeve)

By Satan, never was a hide so thick!	Beim Satan, Er hat eine dicke Haut!
And through the door I'll not let you pass!	Auch dort die Tür passiert Er mir nicht!
I tell you flatly to your face	Ich schrei's Ihm jetzt in Sein Gesicht:
I think you're a rascally knave and a fortune hunter.	Ich acht' Ihn für einen Filou, einen Mitgiftjäger,
You are a scoundrelly liar, and a dirty old peasant,	einen durchtriebenen Lügner und schmutzigen Bauer,
and a cur without honour or shame!	einen Kerl ohne Anstand und Ehr'!
If need be I'll make you learn here and now the truth!	Und wenns sein muss, geb' ich Ihm auf dem Fleck die Lehr'!

Sophie has freed herself from the Baron, and takes refuge behind Octavian. They stand on the left, almost in front of the door.

BARON
(puts two fingers in his mouth and gives a shrill whistle.)

This little boy of ours at seventeen has learned a pretty turn of speech.	Was so ein Bub in Wien mit siebzehn Jahr schon für ein vorlaut Mundwerk hat!

(looking towards the centre door)

But God be praised that everyone in Vienna	Doch Gott sei Lob, man kennt in hiesiger Stadt
knows just who I am,	den Mann, der vor Ihm steht,
and that includes, of course, Her Majesty the Queen!	halt bis hinauf zu kaiserlicher Majestät!
One is just what one is, and there's no need to prove it.	Man ist halt, was man ist, und braucht's nicht zu beweisen.
Now that we understand one another you'll let me pass.	Das lass Er sich gesagt sein und geb mir den Weg da frei.

(All Lerchenau's servants have marched in through the centre door. The Baron, glancing to the back once more, assures himself of their presence. He approaches Sophie and Octavian, determined to secure both Sophie and his retreat.)

I would be most upset if we were forced to teach you—	Wär' mir wahrhaftig leid, wenn meine Leut' dahinten—

92

OCTAVIAN

(furious)

So you have made your mind up to seek help from your grooms and lackeys in our affair. Then draw, sir, or commend your soul!	Ah, untersteh' Er sich, seine Bedienten hineinzumischen in unsern Streit! Jetzt zieh' Er oder gnad' Ihm Gott!

(He draws his sword. The Baron's servants, who had already approached a few steps, hesitate when they see what is happening, and pause in their advance. The Baron takes a step to secure Sophie.)

Draw, damn you, Satan, or on my sword I'll spit you!	Zum Satan, zieh' Er oder ich stech' Ihn nieder!

SOPHIE

Ah, God, oh what will happen next?	Ach Gott, was wird denn jetzt geschehn?

BARON

(withdraws a step)

Before a lady, shame! Are you completely mad?	Vor einer Dame, pfui! So sei Er doch gescheit!

Octavian rushes at him furiously. The Baron draws, lunges clumsily, and receives the point of Octavian's sword in his arm, above the elbow. All the Baron's servants rush on Octavian. He springs aside to the right and keeps them at arm's length, whirling his sword about him. The Almoner, Valzacchi and Annina hurry to the Baron, and, supporting him, lead him to one of the chairs in the middle of the room.

BARON

(dropping his sword)

Help! Help! I'm cut, I'm bleeding! Murder! Murder! Murder!	Mord! Mord! mein Blut! zu Hilfe! Mörder! Mörder! Mörder!

(surrounded by his servants and the Italians, who hide him from the audience)

I'm losing lots of blood! Go, call a doctor!	Ich hab ein hitzig Blut! Um Ärzt'! Um Leinwand!
Some bandage! Call the police! I . . . I'm bleeding to death, to death!	Verband her! Um Polizei, um Polizei! Ich verblut mich auf eins, zwei, drei!
Don't let him go! Call the police! Call the police!	Aufhalten den! Um Polizei! Um Polizei!

LERCHENAU'S SERVANTS

(closing around Octavian with more swagger than courage)

Lay hold there! Lay hold there!	Den haut's z'samm! Den haut's z'samm!
Bandages! Get a sponge!	Spinnweb her! Feuerschwamm!
Quick, take his sword away!	Reisst's ihm den Spadi weg!
Stick him dead, through the heart!	Schlagt's ihn tot auf'm Fleck!

All Faninal's servants, female domestics, kitchen staff, and stable hands, have streamed in through the centre door.

ANNINA

(haranguing the servants)

Yes, zis young gentleman and ze lady, understand? Vere already in secret familiar, understand?	Der junge Kavalier und die Fräulein Braut, versteht's? waren im geheimen schon recht vertraut, versteht's?

Valzacchi and the Almoner divest the Baron of his coat. The latter groans uninterruptedly.

FANINAL'S SERVANTS

Somebody wounded? Who?	G'stochen is einer? Wer?
The stranger there?	Der dort? Der fremde Herr?
Which one? The son-in-law?	Welcher? Der Bräutigam?
Seize the brawler, hold him tight!	Packt's den Duellanten z'samm!
Who is it that first did draw?	Welcher is der Duellant?
That one all dressed in white!	Der dort im weissen G'wand?
Who, the Count that brought the rose?	Wer? Der Rosenkavalier?
For what cause, then? Just for her!	Wegen was denn? Wegen ihr!
Hold him tight! Tan his hide!	Wegen der Braut?
Just for the bride?	Wegen der Liebschaft!
They were a-courting!	Angepackt! Niederg'haut!

	Wütender Hass is'!
We'll make him rue it!	Schaut's nur die Fräulein an,
Look at the brazen thing!	schaut's wie sie blass is!
How dared she do it?	

MARIANNE
(clearing a way for herself to the Baron. All press around him)

| Such a high-born Lord! Such a cruel sword! | So ein fescher Herr! So ein gross' Malheur! |
| Such a heavy blow! Such an awful day! | So ein schwerer Schlag! So ein Unglückstag! |

OCTAVIAN
(holding his assailants at arm's length)

Short shrift for all who	Wer mir zu nah kommt,
come too near to me!	der lernt beten!
I will explain all	Was da passiert ist,
when you can hear me!	kann ich vertreten!

SOPHIE
(from left)

Oh, what confusion is this!	Alles geht durcheinand'!
Wondrous! Quicker than lightning	Furchtbar war's, wie ein Blitz,
he drove them all away!	wie er's erzwungen hat!
I feel naught but the thrill	Ich spür' nur seine Hand,
of his embraces still!	die mich umschlungen hat!
I feel nothing of fear,	Ich verspür' nichts von Angst,
I feel nothing of shame;	ich verspür' nichts von Schmerz,
his bright glances have consumed	nur das Feuer, seinen Blick
all my heart with their flame!	durch und durch, bis ins Herz!

LERCHENAU'S SERVANTS
(desisting from attacking Octavian, they go up to the maids nearest them, whom they proceed to handle roughly)

Linen bands we're needing!	Leinwand her! Verband machen!
Sponges to staunch the bleeding!	Fetzen aus'm G'wand machen!
Bring us quickly salve and plaster,	Vorwärts, keine Spanponaden,
bring them quick for our dear Master!	Leinwand her für Seine Gnaden!

SOPHIE
(calling in despair to Octavian)

| Dearest! | Liebster! |

OCTAVIAN
(calling in despair to Sophie)

| Dearest! | Liebste! |

Faninal rushes in through the door to the left, followed by the Notary and his Clerk, who remain standing by the door in great alarm. Lerchenau's Servants make as if to tear the clothes off the younger and prettier maidservants near them. Mêlée, until Faninal begins.

BARON
(who can be heard, but hardly seen)

I can see other people's blood unmoved, my	Ich kann ein jedes Blut mit Ruhe seh'n,
own makes me flinch!	
My own makes me flinch! Oh! Oh!	bloss das meinig nicht! Oh! Oh!

(shouting at the Duenna)

| Stop shouting and act for once. Don't stand | So tu Sie doch was G'scheidt's, so rett' |
| and watch me. | Sie doch mein Leben! |

ANNINA
(in front, to the left, curtseying, crossing eagerly over to Faninal)

The gentleman and Miss	Der junge Kavalier
are united, Your Honour.	und die Fräulein Braut, Gnaden,
They have been in secrecy	waren im geheimen
plighted, Your Honour!	schon recht vertraut, Gnaden!
Full of devotion	Wir voller Eifer
and care for Your Honour,	für'n Herrn Baron, Gnaden,
we have kept respectfully	haben sie betreten
watch upon the pair, yes, sir.	in aller Devotion, Gnaden!

Marianne rushes out, and after a brief interlude, returns breathless, laden with linen, followed by two maids with sponges and basins. They surround the Baron and busy themselves about him. Sophie, as soon as she sees her father, runs over to the right, and stands by Octavian's side. The latter sheathes his sword.

MARIANNE
(busy about the Baron)

Such a cruel sword!	So ein gross' Malheur!
Such an awful day!	So ein Unglückstag!

FANINAL
(He is at first speechless. Then he throws his hands over his head and bursts out.)

Dear son-in-law, what's happening here?	Herr Schwiegersohn! Wie ist Ihm denn?
The Saints preserve us!	Mein Herr und Heiland!
What an ill-bred affray, here in my house of all things!	Dass Ihm in mein' Palais das hat passieren müssen!
Has no one fetched the surgeon yet? You rogues, you!	Gelaufen um den Medicus! Geflogen!
Take my ten horses. Ride them all to death!	Meine zehn teuren Pferd zu Tod gehetzt!
How is it none of you mustered the wit to throw yourselves between them? Do I feed	Ja hat denn niemand von meiner Livree dazwischen fahren mögen! Füttr' ich dafür
a whole troop of liveried imbeciles only for disgrace	ein Schock baumlange Lackeln, dass mir solche Schand
to fall on me, and on my brand-new palace too?	passieren muss in meinem neuchen Stadtpalais!

(going up to Octavian)

This is not the behaviour I had expected Your Lordship would affect!	Hätt' wohl von Euer Liebden eines and'ren Anstands mich versehn!

BARON
(groaning)

Oh! Oh!	Oh! Oh!

FANINAL
(turning to the Baron)

Oh, that such blood of priceless pedigree should run to waste like this!	Oh! Um das schöne freiherrliche Blut, was auf den Boden rinnt!

(to Octavian)

O pah! Oh! What a common, vulgar butchery!	O pfui! So eine ordinäre Metzgerei!

BARON

I have blood so young, so full of fire, nothing can staunch it! Oh!	Hab' halt so ein jung und hitzig Blut. Ist nicht zum Stillen! Oh!

FANINAL
(venting his anger on Octavian in restrained irony)

Truly from Your most noble Lordship I ventured to expect	War mir von Euer Liebden hochgräflichen Gegenwart allhier
a better show of birth and breeding!	wahrhaftig einer andern Freud' gewärtig!

OCTAVIAN
(politely)

I beg you to forgive me.	Er muss mich pardonieren.
I am so deeply grieved that this thing should have happened.	Bin ausser Massen sehr betrübt über den Vorfall.
But I am not to blame. I promise in the fullness of time,	Bin aber ausser Schuld. Zu einer mehr gelegenen Zeit
Your Honour will discharge me without sentence;	erfahren Euer Liebden wohl den Hergang
you'll hear from your own daughter's lips.	aus Ihrer Fräulein Tochter Mund.

FANINAL
(controlling himself with difficulty)

It's well, sir. Come now, tell me!	Da möcht ich recht sehr bitten!

SOPHIE
(determined)

As you command me, father. I shall unfold my story.	Wie Sie befehlen, Vater. Werd' Ihnen alles sagen.
My Lord there has not acted as a man of honour.	Der Herr dort hat sich nicht so wie er sollt betragen.

FANINAL
(angrily)

How, of whom do you speak? Of my future son-in-law?

If that is so, I beg you think e'er you speak.

Ei, von wem red't Sie da? Von Ihrem Herrn Zukünft'gen?

Ich will nicht hoffen, wär mir keine Manier.

SOPHIE
(quietly)

It is not so. I cannot give my hand to him.

Ist nicht der Fall. Seh' ihn mit nichten an dafür.

FANINAL
(angrily)

Not give your hand?

Sieht ihn nicht an?

SOPHIE

No more. Look at me and forgive me, dear Papa!

Nicht mehr. Bitt' Sie dafür um gnädigen Pardon.

FANINAL
(first muttering to himself, then breaking out in fury)

Not give your hand! No more. Look and forgive.

He lies there wounded. By her side, that schoolboy.

Sieht ihn nicht an. Nicht mehr. Mich um Pardon.

Liegt dort gestochen. Steht bei ihr. Der Junge.

(breaking out)

Disaster! Broken the marriage of my dreams.

All the prying fools of the district and their jealous wives,

how they will jeer! The surgeon! Quick! What if he dies here!

Blamage! Mir auseinander meine Eh'.

Alle Neidhammeln von der Wieden und der Leimgruben

auf! In der Höh! Der Medikus. Stirbt mir womöglich!

(to Sophie, beside himself with rage)

You marry him!

Sie heirat' ihn!

(The Doctor enters, and proceeds at once to attend to the Baron. Faninal turns to Octavian, changing his anger to obsequious civility out of respect for Rofrano's rank.)

And may I now, in all humility, request

Your Lordship to retire from my poor palace, fast as may be,

and never more to show your face here!

Möcht' Euer Liebden recht in aller Devotion

gebeten haben, schleunig sich von hier zu retirieren

und nimmer wieder zu erscheinen!

(to Sophie)

As for you!

You marry him, and if he bleeds to death, no matter,

marry his lifeless body!

Hör' Sie mich!

Sie heirat' ihn! Und wenn er sich verbluten tät,

so heirat' Sie ihn als Toter!

The Doctor indicates with a reassuring gesture that the wounded man is in no danger. Octavian looks for his hat which had fallen under the servants' feet. A Maid hands it to him with a curtsey. Faninal makes an obeisance to Octavian, of exaggerated civility, but unmistakable meaning. Octavian realizes that he cannot stay, but is longing to say one word more to Sophie; he answers Faninal's obeisance with an equally ceremonious bow. Faninal angrily bows a second, then a third time.

SOPHIE
(hurrying to speak the following words while Octavian is still within earshot. Curtseying)

Marry that man I will not, living, and not dead!

I will lock myself away in my room!

Heirat' den Herrn dort nicht lebendig und nicht tot!

Sperr' zuvor in meine Kammer mich ein!

FANINAL
(bowing angrily to Octavian, who promptly returns the bow)

Ah! Lock yourself in! But I shall have

you dragged into a carriage, Mistress Wilful.

Ah! Sperrst dich ein. Sind Leut' genug im Haus,

die dich in Wagen tragen werden.

SOPHIE
(curtseying again)

I'll jump out from the carriage on my way to church.

Spring' aus dem Wagen noch, der mich zur Kirche fährt!

FANINAL

(same business between himself and Octavian, who always moves a step nearer the door, but cannot tear himself away from Sophie)

Jump out from your carriage? Ha! I'll be at your side,
and hold you till we get there.

Ah! Springst noch aus dem Wagen? Na, ich sitz' neben dir,
und werde dich schon halten!

SOPHIE

(curtseying again)

I promise I shall give the priest 'No',
and not 'Yes' for answer.

Geb' halt dem Pfarrer am Altar
Nein anstatt Ja zur Antwort!

In the meantime the Major-Domo dismisses the servants. The stage is gradually cleared. Only Lerchenau's servants remain with their Master.

FANINAL

(same business)

Ah! Give 'No' and not 'Yes' for an answer!
I'll shut you in a convent as I stand here!
Go! Get you from my sight, Miss. Better now than next day!
For all your life!

Ah! Gibst Nein anstatt Ja zur Antwort!
Ich steck dich in ein Kloster stante pede!
Marsch! Mir aus meinen Augen! Lieber heut als morgen!
Auf Lebenszeit!

SOPHIE

(terrified)

I beg you to forgive me! I am not really bad!
Forgive me, I pray you, for just this once!

Ich bitt' Sie um Pardon! Bin doch kein schlechtes Kind!
Vergeben Sie mir nur dies eine Mal!

FANINAL

(furious, shutting his ears)

For all your life! For all your life!

Auf Lebenszeit! Auf Lebenszeit!

OCTAVIAN

(quickly, in an undertone)

Only be calm, beloved, I beg you!
You'll hear from me!

Sei Sie nur ruhig, Liebste, um Alles!
Sie hört von mir!

The Duenna pushes Octavian towards the door.

FANINAL

For all your life!

Auf Lebenszeit!

MARIANNE

(drawing Sophie with her over to the right)

Go, hussy, get you from your father's presence!

So geh doch nur dem Vater aus den Augen!

She pushes her through the door on the right and closes it. Octavian has left by the left-hand door. The Baron is surrounded by his servants, the Duenna, two Maids, the Italians, and the Doctor. He is reclining on a couch made up from chairs, and now can be seen quite clearly.

FANINAL

(shouting once more through the door by which Sophie left)

For all your life!

Auf Lebenszeit!

(hurrying over to the Baron)

I kiss your hand, Sir. O my dear Baron, I embrace you!

Bin überglücklich! Muss Euer Liebden embrassieren!

BARON

(hurt in the arm by the embrace)

Oh! Oh! Jesus Maria!

Oh! Oh! Jesus Maria!

FANINAL

(to the right, his rage increasing again)

Jezebel! To a convent!

Luderei! In's Kloster!

(towards the centre door)

Into prison!
For all your life!

Ein Gefängnis!
Auf Lebenszeit!

BARON

All right! All right! A drop of something liquid.

Is gut! Is gut! Ein Schluck von was zu trinken!

FANINAL

Some wine? Some beer? Some hippocras with ginger?

Ein Wein? Ein Bier? Ein Hippokras mit Ingwer?

(The Doctor makes a nervous, deprecating gesture; Faninal continues, lamenting)

Such noble blood! So patient in misfortune! Such noble blood

So einen Herrn zurichten miserabel,

and in my palace too! You'll marry him, so much the sooner!

in meinem Stadtpalais! Sie heirat' Ihn um desto früher!

I'm master here!

Bin Manns genug!

BARON
(wearily)

All right, all right!

Is gut, is gut!

FANINAL
(towards the left-hand door, his anger flaring up again)

I'm master here!

Bin Manns genug!

(to the Baron)

I kiss your hand for such polite indulgence.

Küss Ihm die Hand für Seine Güt' und Nachsicht.

I am yours to command—I'll run and bring you—

Gehört alls Ihm im Haus. Ich lauf—ich bring' Ihm—

(to the right)

A convent is too good!

ein Kloster ist zu gut!

(to the Baron)

Be at your ease.

Sei'n ausser Sorg'.

(very obsequiously)

I know what true satisfaction shall come from me.

Weiss was ich Satisfaktion Ihm schuldig bin.

He rushes off. The Duenna and the Maids leave at the same time. The two Italians have slunk off during the preceding action. The Baron is left alone with his servants and the Doctor. Soon a footman comes with a carafe of wine, and offers it to the Baron.

BARON

Here am I. What accidents befall a man of quality

Da lieg' ich! Was einem Kavalier nit all's passieren kann

in this old Vienna town.

in dieser Wienerstadt!

I do not like it here. There's no one you can trust save God Himself.

Wär' nicht mein Gusto hier—da ist eins gar zu sehr in Gottes Hand,

I'd rather be at home!

wär' lieber daheim!

(He tries to drink and makes a movement which hurts.)

Oh! Oh! The devil! Oh! Oh! A plague upon that boy!

Oh! Oh! Der Satan! Oh! Oh! Sakerments-verfluchter Bub!

Not yet dry behind the ears, and plays with swords already.

Nit trocken hinter'm Ohr und fuchtelt mit'n Spadi!

(with increasing anger)

Insolent scurvy dog! Wait, wait until I catch you. I'll kill you.

Wällischer Hundsbub' das! Dich sollt' ich nur erwischen,

I swear I'll throw you in with the dogs to cool your heels.

in Hundezwinger sperr' ich dich ein, bei meiner Seel',

In the chicken-coop, no, no, the pigsty. That's where I'll put you! I'll make you hear the angels sing!

in Hühnerstall'! In Schweinekofen! Tät dich kuranzen! Sollst alle Engel singen hör'n!

LERCHENAU'S SERVANTS*

(At once assuming a very dangerous and threatening attitude, turning to the door by which Octavian left.)

We will do for you,
beat you black and blue,
wait, our time will come,
vile Italian scum!

Wenn ich Dich erwisch',
Du liegst unter'm Tisch.
Wart', Dich richt' ich zu,
wällischer Filou!

BARON
(to Faninal's Footman who is waiting on him)

Give me some more wine, quick!

Schenk' Er mir ein da, schnell!

---

* See title page note.

98

(The Doctor pours it out for the Baron and gives it to him. As he drinks his humour gradually returns.)

I can't help laughing just to think what fancies	[12]	Und doch, muss lachen, wie sich so ein Loder
a boy like that can have, he gives himself such airs:		mit seinen siebzehn Jahr die Welt imaginiert:
seems to think he can arrange my affairs.		meint, Gott weiss, wie er mich contreveniert.
Haha! Well, we'll see who laughs the longest! Not for worlds, though,		Haha! umgekehrt ist auch gefahren! Möcht' um all's nicht,
would I have missed the chance to see	[33]	dass ich dem Mädel sein rebellisch
that saucy baggage spitting fire at me!		Aufbegehren nicht verspüret hätt'!
There's nothing I know that excites me so much,		'sgibt auf der Welt nichts, was mich so enflammiert
or that renews my youth so well, as a defiant wench!		und also vehement verjüngt, als wie ein rechter Trotz!

LERCHENAU'S SERVANTS
(in hollow voices)

We will do for you,	Wart', Dich hau' i z'samm,
vile Italian cur,	wällischer Filou,
we will do for you,	wart', Dich hau' i z'samm,
beat him black and blue!	dass Dich Gott verdamm'!

BARON
(turning to the Doctor)

Herr Doctor, go before me to my room!	Herr Medicus, verfüg' Er sich voraus!
And make my bed, of softest feather bedding!	Mach Er das Bett aus lauter Federbetten.
I'll come, but first another drink.	Ich komm'. Erst aber trink' ich noch.
Now off with you, good doctor.	Marschier' Er nur indessen.

(He empties the second cup. Annina has entered through the ante-room, and approaches him discreetly, a letter in her hand. Quietly, to himself.)

A feather bed. Two hours before we dine. I'll die of boredom.		Ein Federbett. Zwei Stunden noch zu Tisch. Werd' Zeitlang haben.
'Without me, without me, lonely days feel all wrong.	[31]	'Ohne mich, ohne mich, jeder Tag dir so bang;
With me, with me, not a night is too long'.		mit mir, mit mir, keine Nacht dir zu lang.'

(Annina places herself so that the Baron cannot avoid seeing her, and makes mysterious signs with the letter.)

For me?	Für mich?

ANNINA
(approaching)

From one you know of.	Von der Bewussten.

BARON

And who, pray, may that be?	Wer soll damit g'meint sein?

ANNINA
(coming quite close to him)

To your hands only, and in secret can I give it.	Nur eigenhändig, insgeheim, zu übergeben.

BARON

Off now!	Luft da!

(His servants retire, unceremoniously taking the carafe from Faninal's Footman and emptying it.)

Give it to me!	Zeig Sie den Wisch!

(He opens the letter with his left hand, tries to read it, holding it far from his eyes.)

Look for my glasses here in my pocket.	Such' Sie in meiner Tasch' meine Brillen.

(very suspiciously, as she is searching)

No! Better not. If you can read, let's hear it.	Nein: Such' Sie nicht! Kann Sie Geschrieb'nes lesen?
There!	Da.

ANNINA
(taking it and reading it)

'Herr Cavalier! Tomorrow come evening I'll be free.	'Herr Kavalier! Den morgigen Abend hätt' i frei.

99

I liked you at once, but I
was too shy there before Her Highness,
'cos I am only a young girl. Your most
  loving Mariandel,
humble serving girl and sweetheart.
Hoping Herr Cavalier has not completely
  forgotten me.
I wait an answer.'

Sie ham mir schon g'fall'n, nur g'schamt
hab i mi vor der Fürstli'n Gnade,
weil i noch gar so jung bin. Das bewusste
  Mariandel,
Kammerzofel und Verliebte.
Wenn der Herr Kavalier den Namen nit
  schon vergessen hat.
I wart' auf Antwort.'

BARON
(delighted)

She waits an answer.
It works like a charm, just like home,
but better with an extra flavour that's new.

Sie wart' auf Antwort.
Geht all's recht am Schnürl, so wie z'Haus'
und hat noch einen andren Schick dazu.

(very merry)

I still have all the luck of the Lerchenaus.

Ich hab' halt schon einmal ein Lerchenauisch Glück.

Come back tonight, I'll give the answer
and in writing.

Komm' Sie nach Tisch, geb' Ihr die
  Antwort nachher schriftlich.

ANNINA

Yours to command, Herr Cavalier.
You won't forget your servant?

Ganz zu Befehl, Herr Kavalier. Vergessen
nicht die Botin?

BARON
(not hearing)

'Without me, without me, lonely days are
  so long'.

'Ohne mich, ohne mich, jeder Tag dir so
  bang.'

ANNINA
(more insistently)

You won't forget your servant, Your
  Highness?

Vergessen nicht der Botin, Euer Gnade?

BARON

All right.
'With me, with me, not a night is too
  long.'

Schon gut.
'Mit mir, mit mir, keine Nacht dir zu
  lang.'

(Annina makes another begging gesture.)

Not just now. All together when it's done.

Das später. Alls auf einmal. Dann zum
  Schluss.

She waits an answer. In the meanwhile,
  leave me.
When you come, bring me a pen and ink,
  and I will
think of an answer to dictate!

Sie wart' auf Antwort! Tret' Sie ab indessen.

Schaff' Sie ein Schreibzeug in mein
  Zimmer hin, dort drüben,
dass ich die Antwort dann diktier'.

*(Exit Annina, not without indicating by a threatening gesture behind the Baron's back that she will
soon be even with him for his niggardliness. The Baron takes a last sip of wine.)*

'With me, with me, not a night is too
  long!'

'Mit mir, mit mir, keine Nacht dir zu
  lang!'

Exit slowly, and quite at his ease, accompanied by his servants.

The curtain falls slowly.

Act Three

Introduction and Pantomime. A private room in an inn. At the back, to the left, a recess, with a bed in it. The recess separated from the room by a curtain, which can be drawn. In the centre, towards the left, a fire-place, with a fire; over it a mirror. In front on the left stands a large, many-branched candlestick. At the back, in the centre, a door leading to the corridor. Next to it on the right, a sideboard. Right back, a blind window; in front, on the right, a window looking onto the street. Candelabra with candles on the sideboard and on the chimney-piece. The room is in semi-darkness. Annina discovered, dressed as a lady in mourning. Valzacchi is arranging her veil, putting her dress to rights, takes a step backwards, surveys her, takes a crayon from his pocket and paints her eyes.

The door on the left is opened cautiously, a head appears, and then vanishes. Then a not unsuspicious-looking, but decently dressed, old woman slips in, opens the door silently, and respectfully introduces Octavian, in female clothes, with a cap, such as girls of the middle-classes wear. Octavian, followed by the old woman, moves towards the two others. Valzacchi is at once aware of them, stops what he is doing, and bows to Octavian. Annina does not at once recognize him in his disguise. She cannot restrain her astonishment, and curtsies low. Octavian feels in his pocket (not like a woman, but like a man, and one sees that under his skirt he is wearing riding-boots and spurs) and throws a purse to Valzacchi. Valzacchi and Annina kiss his hand. Annina puts a finishing touch to his kerchief. Five suspicious-looking men enter, very cautiously, from the left. Valzacchi makes a sign to them to wait. They stand at the left, near the door. A clock strikes the half-hour. Valzacchi takes out his watch, shows it to Octavian; it is high time. Octavian hurries out to the left, followed by the old woman, who acts as his duenna. Valzacchi leads the suspicious-looking men to the front, impressing on them with every gesture the necessity of extreme caution. They follow him on tiptoe to the centre. Annina goes to the mirror (all the while carefully avoiding making a noise), completes her disguise, then draws from a pocket a piece of paper, from which she seems to be learning a part. Valzacchi signals to one of the suspicious-looking men to follow him noiselessly, quite noiselessly. He leads him to the wall on the right, noiselessly opens a trap-door, not far from the table, makes the man descend, closes the trapdoor again, then summons two others to his side, slinks in front of them to the door of the room, puts his head out, assures himself that they are unobserved, makes a sign to them to appear to him, and lets them out. Then he closes the door, directs the two remaining men to precede him silently to the door leading to the side-room, and pushes him out. He beckons to Annina to come to him, goes out with her silently, noiselessly closes the door behind him, and then returns. He claps his hands. The man who is hidden rises to his waist from the trap-door. At the same moment heads appear above the bed and in other places. At a sign from Valzacchi they disappear as suddenly—the secret panels close without a sound.[36] Valzacchi looks again at his watch, goes to the back, opens the door. Then he produces a tinder-box and busily lights the candles on the table. A waiter and a boy run in with tapers for lighting candles. They light the candles on the chimney, on the side-board, and the numerous sconces. They have left the door open behind them; dance music is heard from the ante-room at the back. [16, 37, 38, 39]

Valzacchi hurries to the centre doors, opens them both respectfully, and bowing low steps aside. Baron Ochs appears, his arm in a sling, leading Octavian by his left, followed by his Body-Servant. The Baron surveys the room. Octavian looks around, runs to the mirror, arranges his hair. The Baron notices the Waiter and the Boy about to light more candles, and signals them to stop. In their preoccupation they do not notice him. The Baron impatiently pulls the Boy from the chair onto which he had climbed, and extinguishes some of the candles nearest him with his hand. Valzacchi discreetly points out the recess to him and, by opening the curtains, the bed.

The Landlord hurries forward with several waiters to greet their noble guest.

LANDLORD

What can my poor house still offer Your Lordship?   Hab'n Euer Gnaden noch weitre Befehle?

FOUR WAITERS

A few more candles?   Befehl'n mehr Lichter?

LANDLORD

A better apartment?   Ein grösseres Zimmer?

WAITERS

A few more candles for My Lord?   Befehl'n mehr Silber* auf dem Tisch?
More silver?   Mehr Silber?

---

* 'Lichter' in the vocal score but not in the full score.

BARON

(busily occupied with a napkin which he has taken from the table and is using to extinguish all the candles which he can reach)

Be off! Or you will give the girl ideas!　　Verschwindt's! Macht mir das Madel net
　　　　　　　　　　　　　　　　　　　　　　verruckt!
Who asked for music? Didn't order that.　　Was will die Musi? Hab' sie nicht bestellt.

(putting out more candles)

LANDLORD

Shall they be told to come and play in here?　　Schaffen vielleicht, dass man sie näher hört?
And while you dine they'll play some music.　　Im Vorsaal da is Tafelmusi!

BARON

Leave your damned fiddlers where they are.　　Lass Er die Musi, wo sie ist.

(noticing the blind window on the right behind the table)

That's an odd sort of window there.　　Was ist das für ein Fenster da?

(trying to open it)

LANDLORD

It's only sham, My Lord.　　Ein blindes Fenster nur.

(bows)

Your Lordship's supper waits.　　Darf aufgetragen werd'n?

All five waiters make as if to hurry off.

BARON

Stop! What do these black beetles want?　　Halt, was woll'n die Maikäfer da?

WAITERS
(at the door)

We wait on Your Lordship.　　Servier'n, Euer Gnaden.

BARON
(making a sign for them to go)

I don't need help.　　Brauch' niemand nicht.

(when they hesitate; roughly)

Off now! My servant shall do all the waiting　　Packt's Euch! Servieren wird mein
on;　　　　　　　　　　　　　　　　　　　　　　Kammerdiener da,
and I shall do the pouring. You follow?　　einschenken tu' ich selber. Versteht Er?

(Valzacchi signals to them to respect His Lordship's wish without demur. He pushes them all out of the door. The Baron again begins to extinguish a number of candles, among them some high on the wall, which he can only reach with difficulty; to Valzacchi)

You are a worthy fellow. If you can get　　Er ist ein braver Kerl. Wenn Er mir hilft,
　the bill reduced a little,　　　　　　　　　　die Rechnung runter drucken,
something will come your way. I'm sure　　dann fallt was ab für Ihn. Kost' sicher hier
　it costs a fortune here.　　　　　　　　　　ein Martergeld.

Exit Valzacchi, bowing low. Octavian has now finished. The Baron leads him to a table, they sit down. The Body-Servant by the sideboard contemplates the development of the tête-à-tête with insolent curiosity. He places bottles of wine from the sideboard on the table. The Baron pours out wine. Octavian sips. The Baron kisses Octavian's hand. Octavian withdraws his hand. The Baron signals to the lackey to withdraw, but has to repeat the signal several times before he goes.

OCTAVIAN
(pushes back his glass)

No, no, let be! No wine for me.　　[40] Nein, nein, nein, nein! I trink' kein Wein.

BARON

My dearest, what's this? Come, don't let's　　Geh', Herzerl, was denn? Mach' doch keine
　be silly.　　　　　　　　　　　　　　　　　　Faxen.

OCTAVIAN

No, no, no, no, I have to go.　　Nein, nein, i bleib' net da.

He jumps up as if he was about to go.

BARON
(seizing him with his left hand)

You drive me to despair.　　Sie macht mich deschparat.

OCTAVIAN

I know, Sir, what you think. Oh, you　　Ich weiss schon, was Sie glaub'n. Oh Sie
　naughty man!　　　　　　　　　　　　　　　schlimmer Herr!

BARON
(very loud)

Lord strike me down! I swear by all the
patron saints!

Saperdipix! Ich schwör' bei meinem
Schutzpatron!

OCTAVIAN
(feigns great terror; he runs—as if by mistake—instead of to the door, into the recess, tears the curtains apart, and sees the bed. He pretends to be utterly astonished, and returns in consternation on tiptoe.)

Jesus Maria, there's a bed there, a blooming
great big one.
Cor, blimey, who's it for?

Jesus Maria, steht a Bett drin, a
mordsmässig grosses.
Ja mei, wer schlaft denn da?

BARON
(leading him back to the table)

You'll know in good time. Come on now.
Sit here with me.
He'll soon bring us our supper. Nothing
wrong with your appetite?

Das wird Sie schon seh'n. Jetzt komm'
Sie. Setz' Sie sich schön.
Kommt gleich wer mit'n Essen. Hat Sie
denn keinen Hunger nicht?

The Baron puts his arm around his waist.

OCTAVIAN
(casting languishing looks at the Baron)

O Lord! What a way for a bridegroom to
act.

O weh, wo Sie doch ein Bräut'gam tun
sein.

He pushes him off.

BARON

Oh, can't you for once leave that word
alone.
You sit here with a cavalier at your side,
not with a candlestick maker:
a cavalier leaves all
that is not quite to his taste
outside there by the door. Here sits no
bridegroom;
there sits no lowly chambermaid:
here sits at supper a man in love with his
beloved by his side.

Ach lass Sie schon einmal das fade Wort!

Sie hat doch einen Kavalier vor sich
und keinen Seifensieder:
Ein Kavalier lässt alles,
was ihm nicht konveniert,
da draussen vor der Tür. Hier sitzt kein
Bräutigam
und keine Kammerjungfer nicht.
Hier sitzt mit seiner Allerschönsten ein
[41, 42] Verliebter beim Souper.

(He draws Octavian nearer to him, who leans back coquettishly in his chair, with half-closed eyes. Then he rises. The moment for the first kiss seems to have come. As his face comes close to his companion's, he is violently struck by the likeness to Octavian. He starts backwards, and unconsciously feels his wounded arm.)

That face again! Confounded boy!
He haunts me when I'm dreaming or awake.

Ist *ein* Gesicht! Verfluchter Bub!
Verfolgt mich als a Wacher und im Traum!

OCTAVIAN
(opening his eyes and looking at him with impudent coquetry)

What do you mean?

Was meint Er denn?

BARON

Your face reminds me of a godforsaken boy!

Siehst einem ähnlich, einem gottverfluchten
Kerl!

OCTAVIAN

Go on! I never heard such stuff!

Ah geh! Das hab i no net g'hört!

(The Baron, once again quite certain that it is the chambermaid, forces a smile. But he is not quite free of fear; he has to breathe deeply, and so the kiss is postponed. The man under the trap-door opens it too soon and appears. [36] Octavian, who is sitting opposite him, makes violent signs to him to get out of sight. He vanishes at once. The Baron, taking a few steps to shake off the unpleasant impression, and about to embrace Octavian from behind, catches a last glimpse of him. He is violently alarmed and points to the spot. Octavian continues as if he did not understand.)

What's wrong with you?

Was ist mit Ihm?

BARON
(pointing to the spot where the apparition vanished)

Lord, what was that? Did you see
something more?

Was war denn das? Hat Sie den nicht
geseh'n?

OCTAVIAN

No, not a thing.

Da is ja nix.

BARON

Not a thing?   Da is nix?

(again anxiously scanning Octavian's face)

No?   So?

Nothing there either?   Und da is auch nix?

He passes his hand over his face.

OCTAVIAN

But that's my face.   Da is mei G'sicht.

BARON

(breathing heavily, pouring out a glass of wine)

That is her face—and nothing there—I feel   Da is Ihr G'sicht—und da is nix—mir scheint,
as if I'm going mad.   ich hab' die Kongestion.

He falls heavily into a chair. He is ill at ease. The door is opened, and the music outside can be heard again. [31] The Body-Servant comes in and serves.

OCTAVIAN

(very sentimentally)

What lovely music!   Die schöne Musi!

BARON

(very loud again)

It's my favourite song, you know.   Is mei Leiblied, weiss Sie das?

OCTAVIAN

(listening to the music)

It makes me weepy.   Da muss ma weinen.

BARON

What?   Was?

OCTAVIAN

'Cos it's so lovely.   Weil's gar so schön is.

BARON

What, weeping? Don't be sad.   Was, weinen? Wär' nicht schlecht.
You must enjoy yourself, the music fires the   Kreuzlustig muss Sie sein, die Musi geht
   blood.   ins Blut.

(sentimentally)

Look at me!   G'spürt Sie's jetzt.

(signalling to the servant to go)

Can't you see? Can you not sense   Auf die letzt, g'spürt Sie's dahier,
I've no defence   dass Sie aus mir
and you can make of me your willing   machen kann alles frei, was Sie nur will.
   slave.

The Servant opens the door again, looks in with insolent curiosity, and does not go till the Baron has made an angry sign.

OCTAVIAN

(leaning back, as if speaking to himself, with exaggerated melancholy)

It's all one, it's all one, it's all one,   [43] Es is ja eh alls eins, es is ja eh alls eins,
   it's all one—
All our joys, all our bitter pain.   was ein Herz noch so gach begehrt.

(as the Baron takes his hand)

In the end are they not all in vain?   Geh', es is ja all's net drumi wert.

BARON

(letting go of his hand)

Why, what's this? Oh, they're not all in   Ei wie denn? Is sehr wohl der Müh' wert!
   vain.

OCTAVIAN

(still just as melancholy, casting smouldering glances at the Baron)

As the hours fly by, as the wind blows by,   Wie die Stund' hingeht, wie der Wind
                                 verweht,
so must we too shortly pass away.   so sind wir bald alle zwei dahin.
It's the lot of man,   Menschen sin' ma halt,

(languishing glance at the Baron)

        that we nothing can.   richt'ns nicht mit G'walt.
Not an eye shall weep, nor for your loss,   weint uns niemand nach, net dir net und
   nor for mine.   net mir.

BARON

Is it the wine that makes you so sad? It must be your corset cramps your poor little heart.

Macht Sie der Wein leicht immer so? Is ganz g'wiss Ihr Mieder, das aufs Herzerl Ihr druckt.

(Octavian with closed eyes, gives no answer. The Baron rises and tries to undo his dress.)

I must say I am feeling warm.

Jetzt wird's frei mir a bisserl heiss.

(Without ado he takes off his wig, looking for a place to put it. At that moment he catches a glimpse of a face which appears in the recess and stares at him. The face vanishes in a trice. He says "Brainstorm" to himself, and struggles with his fear, but has to mop his forehead. His eyes again fall on the chambermaid, slumped helplessly on the chair. He is overcome by this, and approaches tenderly. Then he again seems to see Octavian's face close to his own. He starts back again. Mariandl hardly stirs. Once more the Baron wrestles with his fear, forcing himself to put a cheerful face on it. Then his eyes again alight on a strange face, staring at him from the wall. Now he is beside himself with terror: he gives a muffled scream, seizes the hand-bell from the wall and rings it distractedly.)

There, and there, and there, and there!

Da und da und da und da!

(Suddenly the supposedly blind window is torn open, Annina in mourning appears, and points with outstretched arms to the Baron, who is distraught with fear.)

There, and there, and there, and there!

Da und da und da und da!

He tries to protect his back.

ANNINA

My husband! Yes, it is he! 'Tis he!

Er ist es! Es ist mein Mann! Er ist's.

She vanishes.

BARON
(alarmed)

Lord, what was that?

Was ist denn das?

OCTAVIAN

This place is all bewitched.

Das Zimmer ist verhext!

He crosses himself.

ANNINA

(followed by Valzacchi, who makes a pretence of holding her back, rushes in by the centre door, with the Landlord and Three Waiters. Speaking with a Bohemian accent, but in educated tones)

I am his wife! I'll get my hands on him, God is my witness. You be witness also! The law, and the government, Her Majesty, give me back my beloved!

Es ist mein Mann, ich leg' Beschlag auf ihn! Gott ist mein Zeuge, Sie sind meine Zeugen! Gericht! Hohe Obrigkeit! Die Kaiserin muss ihn mir wiedergeben!

BARON
(to the Landlord)

What does this baggage want with me, you fool!

Was will das Weibsbild da von mir, Herr Wirt!

What does he want, and he, and him, and he?

Was will der dort und der und der und der?

(pointing all round the room)

The devil has his home in your God- forsaken private guest room.

Der Teufel frequentier' Sein gottver- fluchtes Extrazimmer.

ANNINA

And would you dare deny me, villain! And make pretence you do not know me?

Er wagt mich zu verleugnen, ah! Tut, als ob er mich nicht täte kennen.

BARON

(He has put a cold compress on his head, holds it in its place with his left hand, then goes right up to the Landlord, the Waiters, and Annina in turn, scanning them closely, as if to convince himself that they are real.)

Alive, by Heaven!

Ist auch lebendig!

(He throws the compress away. Very emphatically)

This baggage, I protest, I never saw before!

Ich hab' wahrhaft'gen Gott das Möbel nie geseh'n!

(to the Landlord)

Begone now, all of you, and let us sup in peace!

Debarassier' Er mich und lass Er fortservier'n!

I vow I'll never more set foot in your low pot-house.

Ich hab' Sein Beisl heut' zum letzten Mal betreten.

ANNINA
(as if only now noticing Octavian's presence)

Ah! It is true, what all my friends did tell me,	Ah! Es ist wahr, was mir berichtet wurde,
that he intends a second marriage, oh the monster,	er will ein zweites Mal heiraten, der Infame,
a second innocent maiden such as I once was.	ein zweites unschuldiges Mädchen, so wie ich es war.

The Landlord is alarmed.

THREE WAITERS

Oh! Your Lordship!	Oh, Euer Gnaden!

BARON

What, am I in a madhouse? Plague on you all!	Bin ich in einem Narrnturm? Kreuzelement!

(He shakes Valzacchi, who is standing next to him, violently.)

Am I Baron Ochs of Lerchenau, tell me, or am I not?	Bin ich der Baron von Lerchenau oder bin ich es nicht?
Am I possessed?	Bin ich bei mir?

(holding a finger in a candle)

Is that a candle,	Is das ein Kerzl,

(brandishing a napkin)

and is that a napkin?	is das ein Serviettl?

ANNINA

Yes, yes, you are he, and as true as you are he,	Ja, ja, du bist es, und so wahr als du es bist,
I am your wife, and you know me full well.	bin ich es auch, und du erkennst mich wohl,
Leupold, Leupold reflect:	Leupold, Leupold bedenk':
Anton von Lerchenau, above us dwells a judge that knoweth all!	Anton von Lerchenau, dort oben richtet dich ein Höherer!

At first he starts violently, so that her speech is interrupted, but she quickly regains her composure.

BARON
(staring at her in bewilderment)

Surely I know you.	Kommt mir bekannt vor.

(looking at Octavian again)

They all have double faces, all of them together.	Hab'n doppelte Gesichter, alle miteinander.

LANDLORD

Poor ill-used lady, wretched, ill-used lady.	Die arme Frau, die arme Frau Baronin!

Four Children between the ages of four and ten rush in, too early, and make for the Baron.

FOUR CHILDREN

Papa! Papa! Papa!	Papa! Papa! Papa!

ANNINA

Hear you the voices of your offspring?	Hörst du die Stimme deines Blutes!
Children, raise your hands to him in prayer!	Kinder, hebt die Hände auf zu ihm!

BARON
(angrily hitting out at the four children with a napkin which he has seized from the table; to the Landlord)

Take all this crew away from here at once.	Debarassier Er mich von denen da,
Take her, take him, and him, and him!	von der, von dem, von dem, von dem!

He points in all directions. Valzacchi meanwhile talks quietly to Octavian.

OCTAVIAN
(to Valzacchi)

Have messengers been sent for Faninal yet?	Ist gleich wer fort, den Faninal zu holen?

VALZACCHI
(whispering)

Ere you 'ad come 'ere. In a moment 'e is 'ere.	Sogleich im Anfang. Wird sogleich zur Stelle sein.

LANDLORD
(whispering behind the Baron's back)

Begging your pardon, go not too far, else it might be the worst for you, harm most serious!	Halten zu Gnaden, geh'n nit zu weit, könnten recht böse Folgen g'spür'n. Bitterböse!

BARON

What? Harm to me from that beldam there? Ne'er have I touched her, not with a pitch-fork's end!	Was? Ich was g'spür'n von dem Möbel da? Hab's nie nicht ang'rührt, nicht mit der Feuerzang'!

ANNINA
(screaming shrilly)

Aah!	Aah!

LANDLORD
(as before)

For bigamy is not a trifle, it is a hanging matter.	Die Bigamie ist halt kein G'spass, is ein Kapitalverbrechen!

VALZACCHI
(softly, to the Baron)

I counsel Your Lordship to 'ave a care. Ze police in zis town, it 'ave no mercy, sir!	Ik rat' Euer Gnaden, sei'n vorsiktig! Die Sittenpolizei sein gar nit tolerant!

BARON

Bigamy? Pooh! A fig for your police!	Die Bigamie? Die Sittenpolizei?

(mimicking the children's voices)

Papa, Papa!	Papa, Papa!

(striking his head as if in despair, then furiously)

Throw out that screaming Jezebel! What, you don't want to? What? Hey, police? Won't they do anything? Are the whole lot of you all in a plot to get me? Are we in Paris? Are we all in a jungle? Or in Her Majesty's own city?	Schmeiss' Er hinaus das Trauerpferd! Wer? Was? Er will nicht? Was? Polizei? Die Lackln wollen nicht? Spielt das Gelichter leicht alls unter einem Leder? Sein wir in Frankreich? Sein wir unter Kurutzen? Oder in kaiserlicher Hauptstadt?

(He pulls open the window looking onto the street.)

Hey police!	Polizei!
Police there, hey, Police! I call you here to help me. Come here, restore some order, come to assist a noble man.	Herauf da, Polizei! Gilt Ordnung her-zustellen und einer Stand'sperson zu Hilf' zu eilen.

Loud cries of 'Police' are heard from the street.

LANDLORD
(lamenting)

Oh! My old inn disgraced! Oh! My good reputation.	Mein renommiertes Haus! Das muss mein Haus erleben!

CHILDREN
(whining)

Papa! Papa! Papa!	Papa! Papa! Papa!

Enter the Commissar of Police with two Constables of the Watch. All stand back to make room for them.

VALZACCHI
(to Octavian)

O Dio! What can we do?	Oh weh, was macken wir?

OCTAVIAN

Have confidence in me and leave the rest to chance.	Verlass' Er sich auf mich und lass' Er's geh'n wie's geht.

VALZACCHI

Your 'umble servant to command!	Zu Euer Exzellenz Befehl!

COMMISSAR
(roughly)

Halt! Keep your places! What is wrong?
Who was it called for help? Who was it broke the peace?

Halt! Keiner rührt sich! Was ist los?
Wer hat um Hilf' geschrie'n? Wer hat Skandal gemacht?

BARON
(going towards him with the self-confidence of a great gentleman)

It's all in order now. I am pleased with your efforts,
just so I'd hoped, everything works like a charm here.

Is alls in Ordnung jetzt. Bin mit Ihm wohl zufrieden.
Hab' gleich erhofft, dass in Wien alls wie am Schnürl geht.

(cheerfully)

Drive all the riffraff away, I wish to dine in private.

Schaff' Er das Pack mir vom Hals; ich will in Ruh' soupieren.

COMMISSAR

And who are you?
What right have you to intervene?
Is this your house?

Wer ist der Herr? Was gibt dem Herrn Befugnis?
Ist Er der Wirt?

(The Baron gapes; the Commissar continues brusquely.)

Then keep a civil tongue and wait a moment,
till I come to question you.

Dann halt Er sich gefällig still
und wart' Er, bis man Ihn vernehmen wird.

(The Baron retires in perplexity, begins to look for his wig, which had disappeared in the confusion, and cannot be found. The Commissar sits down; the two Constables take up their position behind him.)

Who is in charge?

Wo ist der Wirt?

LANDLORD
(submissively)

Pray let me, excellent Sir Constable, only speak for myself, sir.

Mich dem Herrn Oberkommissarius schönstens zu rekommandieren.

COMMISSAR

Your premises do not speak well for you.

Die Wirtschaft da rekommandiert Ihn schlecht!

Now, your report. The whole truth!

Bericht' Er jetzt! Von Anfang!

LANDLORD

Herr Kommissar! His Lordship here—

Herr Kommissar! Der Herr Baron—

COMMISSAR

That great big fat man there? Where have you put your wig, sir?

Der grosse Dicke da? Wo hat Er sein Paruckl?

BARON
(who has been looking for it all this time)

That's what I'm asking you!

Um das frag' ich Ihn!

LANDLORD

That is my Lord, the Baron Lerchenau!

Das ist der Herr Baron von Lerchenau!

COMMISSAR

Then prove it.

Genügt nicht.

BARON

What?

Was?

COMMISSAR

Is there a man of standing here whom you can call as witness?

Hat Er Personen nahebei, die für Ihn Zeugnis geben?

BARON

Right here at hand. There, my secretary, that Italian.

Gleich bei der Hand! Da, mein Sekretär, ein Italiener.

VALZACCHI
(exchanging a glance of understanding with Octavian)

Excuse myself. I not know. He may be a Baron, he may be not. I do not know.

Ick excusier mick. Ick weiss nix. Die Herr kann sein Baron, kann sein auch nit. Ick weiss von nix.

BARON
(beside himself)

This is too much, lying Italian scoundrel!   Das ist doch stark, wällisches Luder, falsches!

The Baron approaches him with his left hand raised.

COMMISSAR
(sharply, to the Baron)

You'd better keep a civil tongue.   Für's erste moderier' Er sich.

OCTAVIAN
(Having stood quietly on the right up till now, runs back and forth as if in despair, unable to find the way out, and mistakes the window for the door.)

Oh my God, I could sink through the floor now!   Oh mein Gott, in die Erd'n möcht' ich sinken!

O Holy Mother of God, you must help me!   Heilige Mutter von Maria Taferl!

COMMISSAR

That young person there, who is she?   Wer ist dort die junge Person?

BARON

She? No one. She stands under my protection here.   Die? Niemand. Sie steht unter meiner Protektion!

COMMISSAR

It's you will soon find some protection very necessary.   Er selber wird bald eine Protektion sehr nötig haben.

Who is the little wench, why is she here?   Wer ist das junge Ding, was macht sie hier?

(looking around)

I've a suspicion that you are one of those abandoned men who lead   Ich will nicht hoffen, dass Er ein gottverdammter Debauchierer

young girls astray! It would go hard with you.   und Verführer ist. Da könnt's Ihm schlecht ergeh'n.

Once more, how come you by her? Answer quickly.   Wie kommt Er zu dem Mädel? Antwort will ich.

OCTAVIAN

Farewell! The river!   I geh' ins Wasser!

Octavian runs through the recess as though to escape, and tears open the curtain, disclosing the peacefully illuminated bed.

COMMISSAR
(rising)

What's this, Landlord, what's this?   Herr Wirt, was seh' ich da?

What business do you carry on?   Was für ein Handwerk treibt denn Er?

LANDLORD
(confused)

When there are persons of rank and fashion—come to dine or sup—   Wenn ich Personen von Stand zum Speisen oder Nachtmahl hab'—

COMMISSAR

Hold you your tongue: wait till I question you.   Halt Er den Mund. Ihn nehm' ich später vor.

(to the Baron)

Now I will count to three, then you must tell me   Jetzt zähl' ich noch bis drei, dann will ich wissen,

how it comes that this honest girl is here with you.   wie Er da zu dem jungen Bürgermädchen kommt.

And I would have you know you had better not deceive me with lying answers.   Ich will nicht hoffen, dass Er sich einer falschen Aussag' wird unterfangen.

The Landlord and Valzacchi indicate with gestures to the Baron how dangerous the situation is and how important his statement is.

BARON
(signalling confidently to them that they may rely on him, and that he was not born yesterday)

The Captain of the Watch, for sure, will think no harm   Wird wohl kein Anstand sein bei Ihm, Herr Kommissar,

if men of quality with their affianced brides   wenn eine Standsperson mit seiner ihm verlobten Braut should choose to sit at supper at nine o'clock here in this inn.

um neune abends ein Souper einnehmen tut.

He glances around him to see the effect of his explanation.

COMMISSAR

She your affianced bride? Then state her father's name
and tell me where he lives. And if you've spoke the truth,
you'll be free with the girl at once to leave us.

Das wäre Seine Braut? Geb' Er den Namen an
vom Vater und's Logis. Wenn Seine Angab' stimmt,
mag Er sich mit der Jungfer retirieren.

BARON

Pray, do you know to whom you speak? I'm not accustomed—

Ich bin wahrhaftig nicht gewohnt, in dieser Weise—

COMMISSAR
(sharply)

Answer without ado, else I will sing quite another tune.

Mach' Er Sein' Aussag' oder ich zieh' andre Saiten auf.

BARON

All right, I'll tell you. This is Mistress Faninal,
Sophie Anna Barbara, daughter to that most distinguished nobleman, Herr von Faninal,
who lives in his palace not far away.

Werd' nicht mankieren. Is die Jungfer Faninal,
Sophia Anna Barbara, eh'liche Tochter des wohlgeborenen Herrn von Faninal,
wohnhaft im Hof im eigen Palais.

The inn-servants, other guests, and some of the musicians from the other room have crowded round the door and are looking on curiously. Herr von Faninal forces a way through them, hastily attired in hat and coat.

FANINAL

The same, sir. What do you want of me?

Zur Stelle! Was wird von mir gewünscht?

(to the Baron)

How strange you look!
I scarce expected you'd desire my presence at this untimely hour here in a common tavern.

Wie sieht Er aus?
War mir vermutend nicht, zu dieser Stunde in ein gemeines Beisl depeschiert zu werden!

BARON
(very astonished and annoyed)

Why have you stuck your nose in? Name of Satan?

Wer hat Ihn hierher depeschiert? In Dreiteufels Namen?

FANINAL
(in an undertone to him)

Why ask me such questions as these, dear son-in-law!
When your excited servants all but broke my door down
to tell me I must come at once and save you from the horrid situation,
in which you find yourself through no fault of yours at all.

Was soll mir die saudumme Frag', Herr Schwiegersohn?
Wo Er mir schier die Tür einrennen lässt mit Botschaft,
ich soll sehr schnell herbei und Ihn in einer üblen Lage soutenieren,
in die Er unverschuldter Weise geraten ist!

The Baron clutches his head.

COMMISSAR

Who is this man? What is he doing here?

Wer ist der Herr? Was schafft der Herr mit Ihm?

BARON

He's not important, only an acquaintance.

He happens to be staying at this inn.

Nichts von Bedeutung. Is bloss ein Bekannter,

hält sich per Zufall hier im Gasthaus auf.

COMMISSAR

Your name, and tell me why you're here!

Der Herr geb' Seinen Namen an!

FANINAL

I am the noble von Faninal.

Ich bin der Edle von Faninal.

COMMISSAR

And this young lady's father?   Somit ist dies der Vater . . .

BARON
(coming between them so as to hide Octavian from Faninal, eagerly)

What he, her father? No, a distant kinsman.   Beileib' gar nicht die Spur. Ist ein Verwandter,
A cousin, it may be. The father is   ein Bruder, ein Neveu! Der wirkliche
full twice as fat as he.   ist noch einmal so dick!

FANINAL
(much astonished)

What means this, pray? How strange you   Was geht hier vor? Wie sieht Er aus? Ich
look. I am her father, surely.   bin der Vater, freilich!

BARON
(trying to draw him aside)

Now leave it all to me, and get you gone.   Das weit're findet sich, verzieh' Er sich.

FANINAL

What, you presume, sir—   Ich muss schon bitten—

BARON

Get you gone, the devil take you.   Fahr' Er heim in Teufels Namen.

FANINAL
(with growing anger)

To drag my name into a vulgar brawl in   Mein Nam' und Ehr in einem solchen
this low tavern!   Händel zu melieren,
I'll not submit!   Herr Schwiegersohn!

BARON
(trying to stop his mouth; to the Commissar)

It is his fancy.   Ist eine idée fixe!
He calls himself so as a joke.   Benennt mich also nur im G'spass!

COMMISSAR

Yes, yes, all right then.   Ja, ja, genügt schon.
(to Faninal)
So you recognize   Er erkennt demnach
this gentleman as your son-in-law?   in diesem Herrn Seinen Schwiegersohn?

FANINAL

Of course, why should I fail to recognize   Sehr wohl! Wieso sollt' ich ihn nicht
him?   erkennen?
Just because he's lost his wig?   Leicht weil er keine Haar nicht hat?

COMMISSAR
(to the Baron)

And you now recognize this gentleman to   Und Er erkennt nunmehr wohl auch in
be,   diesem Herrn
for good or evil, the young lady's father?   wohl oder übel Seinen Schwiegervater?

BARON
(taking the candlestick from the table and holding it up to Faninal's face)

Ha, ha! Well, well! Yes, yes it must be him   Soso, lala! Ja, ja, wird schon derselbe sein.
indeed.
This evening I have not been feeling very   War heut' den ganzen Abend gar nicht
well.   recht beinand'.
I can no longer trust my eyes. I must tell you   Kann meinen Augen heut' nicht trau'n. Muss Ihm sagen,
there's something in this place that gives   liegt hier was in der Luft, man kriegt die
one apoplectic turns.   Kongestion davon.

COMMISSAR
(to Faninal)

You, on the other hand, deny you are the   Dagegen wird von Ihm die Vaterschaft
father
of this girl here who has been described as   zu dieser Ihm verbatim zugeschobenen Tochter
your daughter?   geleugnet?

FANINAL
(noticing Octavian for the first time)

As my daughter? That, that baggage, she says she is a child of mine?

Meine Tochter? Da der Fetzen gibt sich für meine Tochter aus?

BARON
(with a forced smile)

A jest! A mere mistake, I vow! The landlord has told to the Captain of the Watch a tale of me, and how I soon shall wed your daughter.

Ein G'spass! Ein purer Missverstand! Der Wirt hat dem Herrn Kommissarius da was vorerzählt von meiner Brautschaft mit der Faninalschen.

LANDLORD
(in great excitement)

No word, no word from me, 'twas he there that told the story!

Kein Wort! Kein Wort, Herr Kommissarius! Laut eig'ner Aussag'—

FANINAL
(beside himself)

Arrest that shameless baggage! To the prison! I'll have her whipped! I'll have her shut up in a convent! I—I—

Das Weibsbild arretieren! Kommt am Pranger! Wird ausgepeitscht! Wird eingekastelt in ein Kloster! Ich— ich—

BARON

You'd best go home. Tomorrow I will come and tell you all the truth. You know how much you owe to me.

Fahr' Er nach Haus'. Auf morgen in der Früh! Ich klär' Ihm alles auf. Er weiss, was Er mir schuldig ist.

FANINAL
(beside himself with rage)

'Twas you that said it!

Laut eig'ner Aussag'!

(taking a few steps to the rear)

Tell my daughter to come here! Her chair is at the doorway! Bid her come at once!

Meine Tochter soll herauf! Sitzt unten in der Tragchaise! Im Galopp herauf!

(pouncing on the Baron again)

I'll make you pay, sir! I will go to law!

Das zahlt Er teuer! Bring Ihn vor's Gericht!

BARON

What mighty pother you are making now about a little thing. To be your son-in-law a man must have the patience of an ass, parole d'honneur! Now bring my wig here. Find my wig!

Jetzt macht Er einen rechten Palawatsch für nichts und wieder nichts! Ein Kavalier braucht ein' Rossgeduld, Sein Schwiegersohn zu sein! Parole d'honneur! Ich will mei' Perückn!

(shaking the Landlord)

Find me my wig!

Mei' Perückn will ich seh'n!

In his wild hunt for his wig, he seizes some of the children and pushes them aside.

CHILDREN
(automatically)

Papa! Papa! Papa!

Papa! Papa! Papa!

FANINAL
(starting backwards)

Now what is that?

Was ist denn das?

BARON
(He succeeds in finding his hat in his search, and hits out at the children with it.)

Nothing! A swindle! I don't know this baggage! She lies, she says that she's my lawful wife. Damn it to hell! My hands are clean as Pontius Pilate.

Gar nix, ein Schwindel! Kenn' nit das Bagagi! Sie sagt, dass sie verheirat' war mit mir. Käm' zu der Schand' so wie der Pontius ins Credo!

Sophie hurries in in her coat. They make room for her. Faninal's Footmen can be seen through the door, each with a pole of the chair in his hand. The Baron tries to hide his bald pate from Sophie with his hat, while she goes up to her father. [44]

112

ONLOOKERS

The bride! Oh what a sore disgrace!   Die Braut. Oh, was für ein Skandal!

FANINAL
(to Sophie)

Now, look around. See, there your noble   Da schau' dich um! Da hast du den Herrn
suitor stands.   Bräutigam!
And there his gracious Lordship's family!   Da die Famili von dem saubern Herrn!
The wife and all her children! She's his too,   Die Frau mitsamt die Kinder! Da das
                                      Weibsbild
but a morganatic wife! No, that is you,   g'hört linker Hand dazu. Nein, das bist du,
as he himself has said!   laut eig'ner Aussag'. Du!
Does not the same o'erwhelm you? What?   Möcht'st in die Erd'n sinken, was? Ich
Me too.   auch!

SOPHIE
(with a sign of joy)

I'm overjoyed. I never looked on him as   Bin herzensfroh, seh' ihn mit nichten an
mine.   dafür.

FANINAL

Not look on him as yours? Not look on him   Sieht ihn nicht an dafür! Sieht ihn nicht
as yours?   an dafür!
(with growing desperation)
My name and fame! I'll be the mock of   Mein schöner Nam'! Ich trau' mi'
all the city!   nimmer über'n Graben!
I dare not show my face on 'Change again.   Kein Hund nimmt mehr ein Stück'l Brot
                                   von mir.
(almost in tears)

ONLOOKERS
(by the door, in hollow voices)

The disgrace! The disgrace!   Der Skandal! Der Skandal!
For Herr von Faninal!   Für Herrn von Faninal!

FANINAL

I'll never face the town! The scandal   Die ganze Wienerstadt! Die schwarze
paper!   Zeitung!
There! From the cellar! From the air!   Da! Aus dem Keller! Aus der Luft! Die
I'll never face the town!   ganze Wienerstadt!
(to the Baron, clenching his fist)
Oh, you're a rogue! I am not well! A chair!   Oh, Er Filou! Mir wird nicht gut! Ein'
                                   Sessel!

Footmen rush towards him and prevent him from falling. Two of them had previously handed their poles to bystanders. Sophie busies herself about him anxiously. The Landlord also hastens to his aid. They lift him up and carry him into the next room. Several waiters go before them, showing them the way and opening the door. At this moment the Baron catches sight of his wig, which has reappeared as if by magic. He rushes to it, claps it on his head, and sets it straight before a mirror. With this change he regains some of his lost dignity, but he contents himself with turning his back on Annina and the children whose presence makes him uneasy, in spite of everything. The door is closed behind Herr Faninal and his servants. The Landlord and Waiters soon return quietly, fetch drugs, bottles, water and other things, which they carry to the door, and Sophie takes them from them in the doorway.

BARON
(his former self-confidence now completely restored, to the Commissar)

You don't need me any longer. I'll pay,   Sind desto eher im Klaren. Ich zahl', ich
I'll go!   geh'!
(to Octavian)
And now I'll take you home.   Ich führ' Sie jetzt nach Haus'.

COMMISSAR

That's where you're wrong. I have some   Da irrt Er sich. Mit Ihm jetzt weiter im
questions for you still.   Verhör!

At a sign from the Commissar the two Constables remove the bystanders from the room. Only Annina and the children remain standing by the wall on the left.

BARON

Leave well alone now, 'twas a jest, I'll   Lass' Er's jetzt gut sein. War ein G'spass.
tell you later who she truly is.   Ich sag' Ihm später, wer das Mädel ist!

I pledge my word: I'll marry her. I tell you in good time.	Geb' Ihm mein Wort, ich heirat' sie wahrscheinlich auch einmal.
The other one in yonder may go hang.	Da hinten dort, das Klumpret ist schon stad.
You'll know now what I am and what I am not!	Da sieht Er, wer ich bin und wer ich nicht bin!

He is about to lead Octavian off.

OCTAVIAN
(shaking him off)

I will not go with him!	I geh' nit mit dem Herrn!

BARON
(in an undertone)

I'll marry you if you keep well with me.	I heirat' Sie, verhält Sie sich mit mir.
So vastly do you please me, you'll be my Baroness!	Sie wird noch Frau Baronin, so gut gefallt Sie mir!

OCTAVIAN
(freeing himself from the Baron's grip and speaking)

Herr Commissar, I have something to tell you.	Herr Kommissar, ich geb' was zu Protokoll,
But out of the hearing of the Baron.	aber der Herr Baron darf nicht zuhör'n dabei.

At a sign from the Commissar, the two Constables force the Baron to the front right. Octavian seems to be telling the Commissar something which surprises him very much. The Commissar accompanies Octavian to the alcove. Octavian disappears behind the curtains. [43]

BARON
(aside to the Constables, in a familiar tone, pointing to Annina)

God knows who she may be, I swear. We were at supper.	Kenn' nicht das Weibsbild dort, auf Ehr'. War grad beim Essen!
I've not a notion what she wants. That's why I've called you. I've done nothing wrong.	Hab' keine Ahnung, was es will. Hätt' sonst nicht selber um die Polizei—

The Commissar seems to be much entertained, and approaches the curtain without concern.

BARON
(noticing the Commissar's amusement; suddenly much excited by the strange incident)

What is happening there? Can it be possible? The rascal!	Was geschieht denn dort? Ist wohl nicht möglich das? Der Lackl!
No, no, he can't do that to me! She is a maiden! She's a virgin!	Das heisst Ihr Sittenpolizei? Ist eine Jungfer!

(He is restrained with difficulty.)

I am responsible, you see. I warn you.	Steht unter meiner Protektion! Beschwer' mich!
You will pay for this behaviour!	Hab' ein Wörtel dreinzureden!

(He frees himself, and goes towards the recess. They pursue him and seize him again. Mariandel's clothes are throws out of the recess, piece by piece. The Commissar makes a bundle of them. The Baron struggles with his two captors. They have much trouble in holding him, when Octavian's head appears at the opening of the curtains.)

You'd better let me go.	Muss jetzt partout zu ihr!

LANDLORD
(rushing in)

Gentlemen, Her Serene Highness, the Princess von Werdenberg!	Ihre hochfürstliche Gnaden, die Frau Fürstin Feldmarschall!

Enter first servants in the Marschallin's livery, then the Baron's Body-Servant. They form a line. Enter the Marschallin, the little Black Boy carrying her train. [5]

BARON
(He has freed himself from the Constables, and wiping the perspiration from his brow, hurries over to the Marschallin.)

I'm glad beyond all measure. This is more than I deserve.	Bin glücklich über Massen, hab' die Gnad kaum meritiert.
Your intervention here shows me a kindness quite unequalled.	Schätz' Dero Gegenwart hier als ein Freundstück ohne gleichen.

OCTAVIAN
(putting his head out from between the curtains) [1]

Marie Theres', how come you here?	Marie Theres', wie kommt Sie her?

The Marschallin stands motionless, not answering. She looks round with a questioning glance. The Body-Servant, proud and pleased with himself, goes up to the Baron. The Baron indicates his satisfaction with him.

COMMISSAR
(going towards the Marschallin, at attention)

May't please Your Highness, your most humble servant, the Commissary of the district.	Fürstliche Gnaden, melde mich gehorsamst als Vorstadts-Unterkommissarius.

BARON
(at the same time)

You see, Herr Kommissar, Her Highness comes in person to my aid. I think that now you'll know your place.	Er sieht, Herr Kommissar, die Durchlaucht haben selber sich bemüht. Ich denk', Er weiss, woran Er ist.

MARSCHALLIN
(to the Commissar, paying no attention to the Baron)

You know me? And I think I know you too? I think I do.	Er kennt mich? Kenn' ich Ihn nicht auch? Mir scheint beinah'.

COMMISSAR

Yes, well!	Sehr wohl!

MARSCHALLIN

I remember now, you were my husband's orderly?	Dem Herrn Feldmarschall sein' brave Ordonnanz gewest?

COMMISSAR

Yes, Your Highness, to command!	Fürstliche Gnaden, zu Befehl!

Octavian again pops his head through the curtains.

BARON
(Signalling to Octavian to disappear, at the same time in great anxiety lest the Marschallin should notice anything. In an undertone.)

Stay there, confound you, out of sight!	Bleib Sie, zum Sakra, hinten dort!

He hears steps approaching the door on the left to the front, rushes there, and places himself with his back to the door, trying, by means of deferential gestures in the Marschallin's direction, to appear quite at ease. The Marschallin steps over to the left, and looks at the Baron expectantly.

OCTAVIAN
(Coming from behind the curtains in male clothing, as soon as the Baron has turned his back.)

My plan has gone astray, Marie Theres', so strangely.	War anders abgemacht! Marie Theres', ich wunder' mich.

The Marschallin ignores Octavian, and fixes a courteous and expectant look on the Baron, who is dividing his attention, in the utmost perplexity, between the Marschallin and the door. The door on the left is violently opened, so that the Baron, who had been leaning against it in a vain attempt to keep it closed is forced back. Two of Faninal's servants now stand aside to let Sophie pass.

SOPHIE
(not seeing the Marschallin, who is hidden by the Baron)

My father, sir, has asked me to inform you—	Hab' Ihm von mei'm Herrn Vater zu vermelden—

BARON
(interrupting her, in an undertone)

Oh, now is not the time, God damn it all! Will you not wait until I come and call for you? You think that you should be presented in a brothel here?	Ist jetzo nicht die Zeit, Kreuzelement! Kann Sie nicht warten, bis dass man Ihr rufen wird? Meint Sie, dass ich Sie hier im Beisl präsentieren werd'?

OCTAVIAN
(who now comes quietly forward from the alcove, in an undertone to the Marschallin)

That is the lady, she, on whose behalf I—	Das ist die Fräulein—die—um derentwillen—

MARSCHALLIN
(to Octavian, over her shoulder, in an undertone)

You seem a little too concerned, Rofrano. Who she is I can surely guess. She has great charm.	Find' Ihn ein bissl empressiert, Rofrano. Kann mir wohl denken, wer sie ist. Find' sie charmant.

Octavian slips back between the curtains.

(with her back to the door, so angrily that the Baron instinctively starts back a step) [24]

I must inform Your Lordship you'll present me to no one.

For I would have you know I have done with you, once and for all.

Er wird mich keinem Menschen auf der Welt nicht präsentieren,

dieweilen ich mit Ihm auch nicht so viel zu schaffen hab.

(The Marschallin converses in a low tone with the Commissar.)

And this my father bids me tell you: should you carry your

unmannerly presumption only just so far

as to be seen within a hundred yards of where our palace stands,

you'll have yourself alone to thank for what will then befall you.

That, sir, is what my father bids me to say to you.

Und mein Herr Vater lasst Ihm sagen: wenn Er allsoweit

die Frechheit sollte treiben, dass man Seine Nasen nur

erblicken tät' auf hundert Schritt von unserm Stadtpalais,

so hätt' Er sich die bösen Folgen selber zuzuschreiben.

Das ist's, was mein Herr Vater Ihm vermelden lässt.

BARON
(angrily)

Corpo di Bacco!

What a shocking use of disrespectful language!

Corpo di Bacco!

Was ist das für eine ungezog'ne Sprache?

SOPHIE

To match your own.

Die Ihm gebührt.

BARON
(beside himself, trying to pass her and reach the door)

Hey, Faninal, I must—

He Faninal, ich muss—

SOPHIE

Stand back, sir. Do not dare!

Er untersteh' sich nicht!

Faninal's two Footmen come forward, bar his passage, and push him back. Sophie passes through the door, which is closed behind her.

BARON
(shouting through the door)

I'm willing to forget what's happened.

I'll let it be forgiven and forgotten.

Bin willens, alles Vorgefall'ne

vergeben und vergessen sein zu lassen!

MARSCHALLIN
(approaching the Baron from behind, and tapping him on the shoulder.)

Leave well alone now; and go quickly. At once, go.

Lass' Er nur gut sein und verschwind' Er auf eins zwei!

BARON
(turning round and staring at her)

Why should I?

Wieso denn?

MARSCHALLIN
(gaily, sure of victory)

Think of your dignity and take your leave!

Wahr' Er sein' dignité und fahr' Er ab.

BARON
(speechless)

I? What?

Ich? Was?

MARSCHALLIN

Make your 'bonne mine à mauvais jeu'.

And make your exit nobly, like a gentleman.

Mach Er bonne mine à mauvais jeu,

so bleibt Er quasi doch noch eine Standsperson.

The Baron stares at her in amazement. Enter Sophie from the other room, quietly. Her eyes seek Octavian.

MARSCHALLIN
(to the Commissar who has been standing at the back on the right with the two Constables)

You see, Herr Kommissar,

this has all been just a diversion, and nothing more.

Er sieht, Herr Kommissar,

das Ganze war halt eine Farce und weiter nichts.

COMMISSAR

All right then. Respectfully I leave you.

Genügt mir! Retirier' mich ganz gehorsamst.

Exit, followed by the two Constables.

SOPHIE
(aside, frightened)

| This has all been just a diversion and nothing more. | Das Ganze war halt eine Farce und weiter nichts. |

The eyes of the two women meet; Sophie makes an embarrassed curtsey.

BARON
(standing between Sophie and the Marschallin)

| I won't accept it! | Bin gar nicht willens! |

MARSCHALLIN
(impatiently stamping her foot)

| Mon cousin, explain to him. | Mon cousin, bedeut' Er ihm! |

She turns her back on the Baron.

OCTAVIAN
(approaching the Baron from behind, in a very masculine manner)

| Will you permit me? | Möcht' Ihn sehr bitten! |

BARON
(turning sharply towards him)

| Who? What? | Wer! Was? |

MARSCHALLIN
(from the right, where she has now taken up her position)

| Your Lordship, this is Count Rofrano, who then else? | Sein' Gnaden der Herr Graf Rofrano, wer denn sonst? |

BARON
(resignedly, after carefully studying Octavian's face)

| Ah, now I see. | Is schon aso! |

(aside)

That face, it plagues me yet.	Hab' gnug von dem Gesicht.
My eyes did not deceive me then.	Sind doch nicht meine Augen schuld.
It was that boy, then.	Is schon ein Mandl.

Octavian stands there looking insolent and defiant.

MARSCHALLIN
(coming one step closer)

| It was a harmless little masquerade and nothing else. | Is eine wienerische Maskerad' und weiter nichts. |

BARON
(dumbfounded)

| Aha! | Aha! |

SOPHIE
(aside, half sad, half ironically)

| It was a harmless little masquerade and nothing more. | Is eine wienerische Maskerad' und weiter nichts. |

BARON
(aside)

| I see now they were all conspiring to defeat me! | Spiel'n alle unter einem Leder gegen meiner! |

MARSCHALLIN
(haughtily)

| 'Tis well for you it was not really my Mariandel whom you brought into this place here to seduce. | Ich hätt' Ihm nicht gewunschen, dass Er mein Mariandel in der Wirklichkeit mir hätte debauchiert! |

(The Baron is deep in thought as the Marschallin continues, without looking at Octavian.)

| I feel, just now, against all men such a resentment— against all men in general! | [5] Hab' jetzt einen montierten Kopf gegen die Männer— so ganz im allgemeinen! |

BARON
(gradually realizing the situation)

| Well I'll be damned! Now I begin to see it all! | Kreuzelement! Komm' aus dem Staunen nicht heraus! |
| The Feldmarschall—Octavian— Mariandel—the Marschallin—Octavian— | Der Feldmarschall—Octavian— Mariandel—die Marschallin—Octavian— |

117

(with a comprehensive glance, which wanders from the Marschallin to Octavian, and from Octavian back to the Marschallin)

How should I know what I, in my confusion, am supposed to think of this!

Weiss bereits nicht, was ich von diesem ganzen qui pro quo [6] mir denken soll!

MARSCHALLIN
(looking at him fixedly, then more emphatically)

You are surely a cavalier? So you will just refrain from thinking. That is what I from you expect.

Er ist, mein' ich, ein Kavalier? Da wird Er sich halt gar nichts denken. Das ist's, was ich von Ihm erwart'.

BARON
(bowing with the grace of a man of the world)

I am simply delighted and charmed, beyond all measure charmed. No Lerchenauer ever spoiled a little bit of sport.

Bin von so viel Finesse charmiert, kann gar nicht sagen wie. Ein Lerchenauer war noch nie kein Spielverderber nicht.

(coming one step nearer)

I like the way you've played this whole affair. And now I can rely on your assistance and support. As for our little secret, I'm prepared to let it be forgiven and forgotten.

Find' deliziös das ganze qui pro quo, bedarf aber dafür nunmehro Ihrer Protektion: Bin willens, alles Vorgefallene vergeben und vergessen sein zu lassen.

(pause)

Eh bien, may I tell Faninal—

Eh bien, darf ich den Faninal—

He goes to the left-hand door.

MARSCHALLIN

You may—you may without a word retire and leave us.

Er darf, Er darf in aller Still' sich retirieren!

(The Baron is dumbfounded.)

Can you not tell when an affair is ended? [20]

Versteht Er nicht, wenn eine Sach' ein End' hat?

Your talk of marriage, the affair, and everything connected with it

Die ganze Brautschaft und Affär' und alles sonst, was drum und dran hängt,

(very emphatically)

from this hour is at an end.

ist mit dieser Stund' vorbei.

SOPHIE

Connected with it, from this hour is at an end.

Was drum und dran hängt, ist mit dieser Stund' vorbei.

BARON
(aside, very indignant, softly)

Is at an end, an end! Is at an end, an end!

Mit dieser Stund' vorbei! Mit dieser Stund' vorbei!

MARSCHALLIN
(She seems to be looking for a seat. Octavian hurries forward and gives her a chair. The Marschallin sits down on the right. Aside, in a significant tone.)

Is at an end.

[5] Ist halt vorbei!

SOPHIE
(on the left, aside, pale)

Is at an end.

Ist halt vorbei!

The Baron fails to appreciate this new development, and rolls his eyes in anger and perplexity. At this moment the man emerges from the trapdoor. Valzacchi enters from the left, followed by his suspicious accomplices, with modest demeanour. Annina tears off her widow's cap and veil, rubs off her make-up revealing her natural face. The Baron's astonishment grows. The Landlord enters by the centre door, carrying a long bill, followed by waiters, musicians, house boys, and coachmen.

BARON
(As he sees them, he realizes that the game is lost. He calls out quickly and decidedly.)

Leupold, let's go.

Leupold, wir geh'n!

He makes a low, angry bow to the Marschallin. His Body-Servant seizes a candle from the table, and prepares to lead the way for his master. Annina insolently bars the Baron's passage.

ANNINA

I still have all the luck of the
Lerchenaus.

'Ich hab' halt schon einmal ein
Lerchenauisch Glück!'

(pointing to the Landlord's bill)

Come back tonight, I'll give the
answer and in writing.

[31] 'Komm' Sie nach Tisch, geb' Ihr die
Antwort nachher schriftlich!'

The Children run between the Baron's legs. He hits out at them with his hat.

CHILDREN

Papa! Papa! Papa!

Papa! Papa! Papa!

WAITERS
(pressing forward to the Baron)

May't please you, Your Highness!
There are lights to pay!

Entschuld'gen Euer Gnaden!
Uns geh'n die Kerzen an!

LANDLORD
(pressing forward with his bill)

May't please you, Your Highness!

Entschuld'gen Euer Gnaden!

ANNINA
(dancing backwards in front of the Baron)

I still have all the luck of the Lerchenaus.

'Ich hab' halt schon einmal ein
Lerchenauisch Glück!'

VALZACCHI
(ironically)

I still have all the luck of the Lerchenaus!

'Ich hab' halt schon einmal ein
Lerchenauisch Glück!'

MUSICIANS
(barring the Baron's passage)

There's music, two hours and more, sir.

Tafelmusik über zwei Stunden.

The Body-Servant forces a way to the door; the Baron tries to follow him.

COACHMEN
(crowding round the Baron)

For the coach, for the coach. Horses
standing. Time is up!

Für die Fuhr', für die Fuhr'! Rösser
g'schund'n ham ma gnua!

BOOTS
(insolently bawling at the Baron)

Don't forget, sir, I lock the house.

Sö fürs Aufsperr'n, Sö, Herr Baron.

LANDLORD
(still presenting his bill)

May't please you, Your Lordship.

Entschuld'gen Eu'r Gnaden!

WAITERS

Two score candles. There are the lights to
pay.

Zwei Schock Kerzen, uns geh'n die Kerzen
an.

BARON
(in the crowd)

Clear off, clear off, out of my way!

Platz da, Platz da, Kreuzmillion!

BOOTS

I help the coachman, sir, I lock the house.

Führag'fahr'n, aussag'ruckt, Sö, Herr
Baron!

CHILDREN

Papa! Papa! Papa!

Papa! Papa! Papa!

All shout in wild confusion. They reach the door. The candle is wrested from the Body-Servant. The Baron rushes off; all hurry after him. The noise grows fainter. Faninal's two Footmen have gone out by the door on the left. Sophie, the Marschallin, and Octavian are left alone.

SOPHIE
(standing on the left, pale)

Oh God! The story was a masquerade and
no more.
Oh God!
He goes towards her, and I am no more
alive for him.

Mein Gott, es war nicht mehr als eine Farce.

Mein Gott, mein Gott!
Wie er bei ihr steht und ich bin die leere
Luft für ihn.

OCTAVIAN
(behind the Marschallin's chair, embarrassed)

My plan has gone astray, Marie Theres', so strangely!	War anders abgemacht, Marie Theres, ich wunder' mich.

(in extreme embarrassment)

Command me, shall I—should I not—the Lady—her father—	Befiehlt Sie, dass ich—soll ich nicht—die Jungfer—der Vater—

MARSCHALLIN

Go quickly, and do all that your heart commands.	Geh' Er doch schnell und tu Er, was Sein Herz Ihm sagt.

SOPHIE
(in despair)

No more alive! Oh my God! Oh my God!	Die leere Luft. O mein Gott! Mein Gott!

OCTAVIAN

Theres', I do not know—	Theres', ich weiss gar nicht—

MARSCHALLIN

Go now, and pay her your court.	Geh' Er und mach' Seinen Hof.

OCTAVIAN

I swear it—	Ich schwör' Ihr—

MARSCHALLIN

'Tis no matter.	Lass' Er's gut sein.

OCTAVIAN

But I do not understand.	Ich begreif' nicht, was Sie hat.

MARSCHALLIN
(laughing angrily)

How like a man to say that. Go to her!	Er ist ein rechtes Mannsbild, geh' Er hin.

OCTAVIAN

As you command.	Wie Sie befiehlt.

(He goes to her. Sophie stands speechless.)

Eh bien, have you no friendly word for me?	[45] Eh bien, hat Sie kein freundlich Wort für mich?
No glance or smile, no smile to show that you care?	Nicht einen Blick, nicht einen lieben Gruss?

SOPHIE
(hesitating)

Ah, my Lord, I had dared to expect of you and your chivalry a token of affection more than pity.	War mir von Euer Gnaden Freundschaft und Behilflichkeit wahrhaftig einer andern Freud' gewärtig.

OCTAVIAN
(eagerly)

What? Are you not then glad?	Wie—freut Sie sich denn nicht?

SOPHIE
(angrily)

Pray, then tell me what cause I have.	Hab' wirklich keinen Anlass nicht.

OCTAVIAN

Have we not chased that wretch away that made you sad?	Hat man Ihr nicht den Bräutigam vom Hals geschafft?

SOPHIE

It could have been a day of happiness and joy. Yet all conspires to shame me. And in the smile Her Highness turns on me I can feel all the pity and the scorn.	Wär' all's recht schön, wenn's anders abgegangen wär'. Schäm' mich in Grund und Boden. Versteh' sehr wohl, mit was für einem Blick Ihre fürstliche Gnaden mich betracht'.

OCTAVIAN

I swear upon my soul it is not so!	Ich schwör' Ihr meiner Seel' und Seligkeit!

SOPHIE

Pray let me go now!	Lass' Er mich geh'n.

OCTAVIAN

I never shall!	Ich lass' Sie nicht.

(seizing her hand)

	SOPHIE
My father needs my help.	Der Vater braucht mich drin.
	OCTAVIAN
I need you more than he!	Ich brauch' Sie nötiger.
	SOPHIE
It's lightly said.	Das sagt sich leicht.

The Marschallin rises abruptly, but controls herself, and sits down again.

	OCTAVIAN
I love you more than words can say.	Ich hab' Sie übermässig lieb.
	SOPHIE
It is not true.	Das ist nicht wahr.
Your love is not as great as you declare.	Er hat mich nicht so lieb, als wie Er spricht.
Forget me then!	Vergess Er mich.
	OCTAVIAN
You are my all, you are my all!	Ist mir um Sie und nur um Sie!
	SOPHIE
Forget me then!	Vergess Er mich.

	OCTAVIAN
	(vehemently)
The world may vanish for all I care!	Mag alles drunter und drüber geh'n.
	SOPHIE
	(passionately)
Forget me then!	Vergess Er mich.
	OCTAVIAN
I have no thought now, but love for you.	Hab' keinen andern Gedanken nicht.
I see you, your lovely face.	Seh' all'weil Ihr lieb Gesicht.
So dear to me, my love.	Hab' allzulieb Ihr lieb Gesicht.

He takes both her hands in his.

	SOPHIE
	(weakly pushing him away)
Forget me now!	Vergess Er mich.

	MARSCHALLIN
	(aside, at the same time)
Now or tomorrow, if not tomorrow, very soon,	Heut' oder morgen oder den übernächsten Tag.
did I not say the words myself?	Hab' ich mirs denn nicht vorgesagt?
There is no woman can escape this fate.	Das alles kommt halt über jede Frau.
Did I not know the truth?	Hab' ich's denn nicht gewusst?
Did I not take a vow on it?	Hab' ich nicht ein Gelübde tan,
That I with all my heart and humble spirit must bear the blow . . .	dass ich's mit einem ganz gefassten Herzen ertragen werd' . . .
Now or tomorrow, if not tomorrow, very soon.	Heut oder morgen oder den übernächsten Tag.

She wipes her eyes and stands up.

	SOPHIE
	(softly)
The Princess there! She's calling you! Go speak to her!	Die Fürstin da! Sie ruft Ihn hin. So geh' Er doch!

(Octavian takes a few steps towards the Marschallin, and stands in indecision between the two. Pause. Sophie, in the doorway, cannot decide whether to stay or go. Octavian between them turns his head from one to the other. The Marschallin notices his perplexity and a melancholy smile flits across her face.)

I must go in, I think I hear my father call.	Ich muss hinein und fragen, wie's dem Vater geht.
	OCTAVIAN
So much is unspoken, I have no words to speak.	Ich muss jetzt was reden und mir verschlagt's die Red'.
	MARSCHALLIN
Poor boy, look how confused he stands there between us two.	Der Bub, wie er verlegen da in der Mitten steht.

OCTAVIAN
(to Sophie)

By all that's holy, stay. Bleib' Sie um alles hier.

(to the Marschallin)

Yes. What was that you said? Wie, hat Sie was gesagt?

MARSCHALLIN
(She pays no attention to Octavian, but crosses over to Sophie and looks at her critically but kindly. Sophie, much embarrassed, makes a curtsey.)

So quickly have you learned to love   [5] So schnell hat Sie ihn gar so lieb?
him?

SOPHIE
(very quickly)

Indeed, Ma'am, your question I can hardly   Ich weiss nicht, was Euer Gnaden meinen
understand.   mit der Frag'.

MARSCHALLIN

Your cheek so pale gives me the answer   Ihr blass' Gesicht gibt schon die rechte
plain enough.   Antwort drauf.

SOPHIE
(very timid and embarrassed. Still very quickly)

No wonder if my cheeks are pale, Your   Wär' gar kein Wunder, wenn ich blass bin,
Highness.   Euer Gnaden.

I have been dreadfully afraid for my poor   Hab' einen grossen Schreck erlebt mit dem
father,   Herrn Vater.

not to speak also of my anger at all the vile   Gar nicht zu reden von gerechtem Emporte-
   ment

things that that hateful man has said and   gegen den skandalösen Herrn Baron.
done.

I am most grateful, forever grateful to Your   Bin Euer Gnaden in Ewigkeit verpflichtet,
Highness for your help and kindness.   dass mit Dero Hilf' und Aufsicht—

MARSCHALLIN
(deprecatingly)

No need to talk so much. You're pretty,   Red' Sie nur nicht zu viel, Sie ist ja hübsch
that's enough!   genug.

And as for your dear papa's discomfort, I   Und gegen dem Herrn Papa sein Übel weiss
know just the medicine for him.   ich etwa eine Medizin.

I'll go, say a few words to him, and bid him   Ich geh' jetzt da hinein zu ihm und lad'
   ihn ein,

ride with me and you and Count Octavian   mit mir und Ihr und dem Herrn Grafen da,
in my own carriage, we'll go home now—   in meinem Wagen heimzufahren—meint
don't you think   Sie nicht,

that will be quite enough to make him well   dass ihn das rekreieren wird und allbereits
again

and even cheer his spirits?   ein wenig munter machen?

SOPHIE

Ah, Your Highness, you are much too kind.   Euer Gnaden sind die Güte selbst.

MARSCHALLIN

And for your pale cheeks, I think my cousin   Und für die Blässe weiss vielleicht mein
there will have the cure.   Vetter da die Medizin.

OCTAVIAN
(with deep feeling)

Marie Therese, how good you are.   Marie Theres, wie gut Sie ist.
Marie Therese, I wish I knew—   Marie Theres, ich weiss gar nicht—

MARSCHALLIN
(with an enigmatic expression, softly)

I know nothing—   Ich weiss auch nix.

(quite without expression)

Nothing.   Gar nix.

She indicates to him to stay.

OCTAVIAN
(undecided, as if he wished to follow her)

Marie Therese!   Marie Theres!

The Marschallin remains standing in the door. Octavian is beside her, Sophie further off to the right.

122

(aside, at the same time as Octavian and Sophie)

I made a vow to love him rightly, as a [46] Hab' mirs gelobt, ihn lieb zu haben in der
  good woman should,   richtigen Weis',
e'en to love the love he bore another,   dass ich selbst sein' Lieb' zu einer andern
I promised.   noch lieb hab'!
But in truth, I did not think   Hab' mir freilich nicht gedacht,
that all so soon I'd find the task await me.   dass es so bald mir aufgelegt sollt' werden.

(sighing)

Full many a thing is ordained in this world,   Es sind die mehreren Dinge auf der Welt,
which we should scarce believe could be   so, dass sie eins nicht glauben tät',
  if we heard others tell of them.   wenn man sie möcht' erzählen hör'n.
And only we who live them believe in them,   Alleinig wer's erlebt, der glaubt daran und
  and know not how—   weiss nicht wie—
there stands the boy, and here stand I, and   Da steht der Bub und da steh' ich und mit
  with this pretty child of his   dem fremden Mädel dort
he will know happiness such as a man thinks   wird er so glücklich sein, als wie halt
  Männer
the best the world can give. God wills,   das Glücklichsein versteh'n. In Gottes
  so be it.   Namen.

(together with the Marschallin and Sophie, first to himself, then gazing into Sophie's eyes)

Can I believe it has come to pass?   Es ist was kommen und ist was g'scheh'n.
Would I could ask her, 'Can it be?' And just   Ich möcht' sie fragen: Darf's denn sein?
  that question   und grad die Frag',
is the question that I dare not ask.   die spür' ich, dass sie mir verboten ist.
Would I could ask her, why, oh why, why   Ich möcht' sie fragen: Warum zittert was
  am I afraid?   in mir?
What if a cruel wrong has been done? And   Ist denn ein grosses Unrecht gescheh'n?
  yet of her   Und grad an die
I may not ask the question—and then I see   darf ich die Frag' nicht tun—und dann
  you by me,   seh' ich dich an,
Sophie, and see but you, know but you,   Sophie, und seh' nur dich und spür' nur
  dich,
Sophie, and know no more but you: you,   Sophie, und weiss von nichts als nur: dich
  you I love.   hab' ich lieb.

(together with the Marschallin and Octavian, at first to herself, then gazing into Octavian's eyes)

I feel as when I'm kneeling, holy rapture   Mir ist wie in der Kirch'n, heilig ist mir und
  mixed with fear,   so bang
and rapture that's unholy too, I know not   und doch ist mir unheilig auch! Ich weiss
  what I feel.   nicht, wie mir ist.

(with much expression)

I'd gladly kneel before My Lady there,   Ich möcht' mich niederknien dort vor der
  yet I'd hurt her   Frau und möcht' ihr
gladly; for I feel, she gives me him,   was antun, denn ich spür', sie gibt mir ihn
and yet robs me of part of him.   und nimmt mir was von ihm zugleich.
I know not how it is!   Weiss gar nicht wie mir ist.
Could I understand! And yet I fear the truth!   Möcht' alles versteh'n und möcht' auch
  nichts versteh'n.
I would know and yet not know;   Möcht fragen und nicht fragen, wird mir
  I am hot and cold.   heiss und kalt
And know but you, know but this one thing: und spür' nur dich und weiss nur eins:
  that I love you.   dich hab' ich lieb.

The Marschallin goes quietly into the room on the left; the two others do not notice her. Octavian comes close to Sophie. A moment later she is in his arms.)

Bliss is too deep to understand,   [47] Spür' nur dich, spür' nur dich allein
one in happiness and hand in hand!   und dass wir beieinander sein!
Years to come glimmer like the sun   Geht all's sonst wie ein Traum dahin
before my eyes!   vor meinem Sinn!

Am I dreaming that here we stand,   Ist ein Traum, kann nicht wirklich sein,
one in happiness and hand in hand?   dass wir zwei beieinander sein,

Ever hand in hand to be   beieinand für alle Zeit
for all eternity!   und Ewigkeit!

OCTAVIAN

In a palace once upon a day,   War ein Haus wo, da warst du drein
you were waiting till I stole you away.   und die Leute schicken mich hinein,
They let me steal the brightest jewel there,   mich gradaus in die Seligkeit!
fools that they were!   Die waren g'scheit!

SOPHIE

You are laughing? I stand in dread,   Kannst du lachen! Mir ist zur Stell'
such a tumult runs in my head.   bang wie an der himmlischen Schwell'!
Hold me! A weak foolish thing,   Halt mich, ein schwach' Ding wie ich bin,
to you I cling!   sink' dir dahin!

She leans on him for support. At this moment Faninal's Footmen open the door and enter, each carrying a candlestick. Faninal, leading the Marschallin by the hand, enters through the door. The two young people stand for a moment in confusion, then they make a deep bow, which Faninal and the Marschallin return. Faninal pats Sophie on the cheek with paternal benevolence.

FANINAL

It's ever so, youth will be youth!   Sind halt aso, die jungen Leut!

MARSCHALLIN

Ah, yes.   Ja, ja.

Faninal gives the Marschallin his hand, and conducts her to the centre door, which is at that moment thrown open by the Marschallin's suite, among them the little Black Boy. Outside the light is bright, inside it is half-dark, as the two Footmen precede the Marschallin with the candlesticks. Octavian and Sophie are left alone in the darkened room. Dreamily they repeat:

OCTAVIAN

Bliss too deep to understand,   Spür' nur dich, spür' nur dich allein
one in happiness and hand in hand!   und dass wir beieinander sein!
Years to come glimmer like the sun   [29] Geht all's sonst wie ein Traum dahin
before my eyes.   vor meinem Sinn!

Am I dreaming that here we stand,   Ist ein Traum, kann nicht wirklich sein,
one in happiness and hand in hand?   dass wir zwei beieinander sein,
Ever hand in hand to be   beieinand' für alle Zeit
for all eternity!   und Ewigkeit!

BOTH

You are mine alone, you alone.   Spür' nur dich allein.

She sinks into his arms. He kisses her quickly. Her handkerchief drops from her hand without her noticing. Then they run quickly off, hand in hand. The stage remains empty. Then the centre door opens again. The little Black Boy comes in with a taper in his hand, looks for the handkerchief, finds it, and trips out. [9]

The curtain falls quickly.

124

Lotte Lehmann as the Marschallin.

Selective Discography

David Nice

The 1933 recording listed below is a series of excerpts rather than a performance with cuts — though these can be unexpectedly severe, too, in the final Act One confrontation between the Marschallin and Octavian. Erich Kleiber in 1954 preferred his *Rosenkavalier* absolutely complete, and Decca seemed happy to comply, though the result hardly set precedents; of subsequent sets, both of Karajan's and Bernstein's are variously cut. Posterity has nothing of Strauss conducting his opera in the theatre, but the voiceless

Conductor	Weger* (abridged, see note)	E. Kleiber*	Karajan
Orchestra	**VPO**	**VPO**	**Philharmonia**
Date	1933	1954	1957
Marschallin	Lehmann	Reining	Schwarzkopf
Octavian	Olczewska	Jurinac	Ludwig
Sophie	Schumann	Gueden	Stich-Randall
Ochs	Mayr	Weber	Edelmann
Faninal	Madin	Poell	Wächter
Marianne	Michalsky	Hellwig	Welitsch
Valzacchi	Gallos	Klein	Kuen
Annina	Paalen	Rossl-Majdan	Meyer
Italian tenor	—	Dermota	Gedda
CD number	Pearl GEMM CDS 9365 (2) + EMI CHS 7 64487 2 (2)	Decca 425 950-2 (2)	EMI CDS 7 49354 2 (3)

series of excerpts he made, with London's Tivoli Theatre Orchestra, for the 1926 film gives a very good idea of how he preferred to move the set pieces flexibly along. It is available either on Koch Legacy (3-7132-2 HI) or, in slightly better transfers, on EMI CDC 7 546102, coupled in both cases with a 1941 rendering of the Alpine Symphony. Two videos give a fuller picture: one features Solti's interpretation 16 years on from the Decca recording, in the context of John Schlesinger's Royal Opera production (Castle) and the other is the sole testament to Carlos Kleiber's electrifying Strauss conducting in Munich (DG). All recordings listed are currently available on CD only; those asterisked are in mono.

Solti	*Bernstein*	*Karajan*	*Haitink*
VPO	**VPO**	**VPO**	**Dresden Staatskapelle**
1969	1971	1984	1990
Crespin	Ludwig	Tomowa-Sintow	Te Kanawa
Minton	Jones	Baltsa	von Otter
Donath	Popp	Perry	Hendricks
Jungwirth	Berry	Moll	Rydl
Wiener	Gutstein	Hornik	Grundheber
Loose	Loose	Lipp	Faulkner
Dickie	Dickie	Zednik	Clark
Howells	Lilowa	Müller-Molinari	Powell
Pavarotti	Domingo	Cole	Leech
Decca 417 493-2 (3)	CBS CD42564 (3)	DG 423 850-2 (3)	EMI CDS 7 54259 2 (3)

Bibliography

Perceptive discussions of *Der Rosenkavalier* are contained in the major studies in English of Richard Strauss: Norman Del Mar's *Richard Strauss: A critical commentary on his life and works* (Barrie and Rockliff, 3 volumes, 1962-1972; reprinted with corrections, 1978) and William Mann's *Richard Strauss: A Critical Study of the Operas* (Cassell, 1964). Michael Kennedy's volume on the composer for the *Master Musicians* series (Dent, 1976) is the best short introduction to his total output. The fascinating correspondence between Strauss and Hofmannsthal (Collins, 1961; reprinted Cambridge U.P., 1981) is a unique record of the collaboration of a composer and librettist. Alan Jefferson has published several books on Strauss, notably the Cambridge Opera Handbook to this opera. The most recent study of Strauss is the volume dedicated to him by David Nice in the *Illustrated Lives of the Great Composers* series (Omnibus, 1993).

Erté's design for Act Three, Glyndebourne, 1980, in John Cox's production, set around 1850. (© Sevanarts Limited; by courtesy of Erté and the Grosvenor Gallery)